PSYCHOLOGY
AND
ARTHUR
MILLER

Dr. Richard I. Evans is Professor of Psychology and coordinates the graduate social psychology program at the University of Houston. He received his B.S. and M.S. degrees in Psychology at the University of Pittsburgh and his Ph.D. in Psychology at Michigan State University. Under a National Science Foundation grant, he has filmed dialogues with the world's most notable psychologists, including Carl Jung, Erich Fromm, Erik Erikson, and B. F. Skinner, from which the books in this series are derived. He is a pioneer in educational television and the social psychology of communication, and taught the nation's first college course on noncommercial television. His continuing concern with sound public education in psychology has led to frequent appearances on commercial and educational television programs. He has published a number of professional articles in social psychology. His most recent books are *Resistance to Innovation in Higher Education* and *B. F. Skinner: The Man and His Ideas*.

PSYCHOLOGY AND ARTHUR MILLER

RICHARD I. EVANS

E. P. DUTTON & CO., INC.
NEW YORK   1969

First Edition

To my lovely wife and children (including Randy who at fifteen read *The Crucible* as a class assignment and became the first student who used *Psychology and Arthur Miller* as a source) and to Inge Miller for her wonderful comment about the dialogue, "This is *really* Arthur."

ACKNOWLEDGMENTS

In the long process involved in filming and taping the dialogues with Arthur Miller and transcribing, editing, and integrating them into the present volume, I am indebted to a great many individuals. Though space prohibits mentioning everyone who so kindly assisted in this venture, I wish to express my appreciation to at least some of these individuals.

Thanks are accorded Dr. Gerald O'Grady. As an English professor, his vast knowledge of Arthur Miller's work from a literary perspective provided an interesting backdrop as I developed the psychological perspective emphasized in the present volume. Thanks also to Arthur Miller's friend and producer, Robert Whitehead, for writing the preface.

Thanks are also due to Mrs. Martha Frede and Mrs. Merle Levy for their assistance in transcribing the tapes and preliminary editing of the manuscript.

Grateful acknowledgment is made to the University of Houston for permission to utilize the printed texts of the filmed and taped discussion. Mr. James Bauer of the University of Houston, who functioned in the demanding role of technical director of the taping and filming sessions, should also be mentioned among those who have greatly assisted me.

I wish to express my thanks to Miss Miriam Thompson for her patience and skill in typing the manuscript.

I am also grateful for the support from the National Science Foundation, without which this project could not have been implemented.

Finally, the wonderful cooperation of Arthur Miller cannot be emphasized enough. Not only was he willing to participate in the filming and taping sessions which are involved in this project, but in spite of his extremely busy schedule, he was willing to edit and even in some instances amend the text of the material in printed form, so that this volume would not suffer in the transition from film and sound to print.

Richard I. Evans
Professor of Psychology
University of Houston

CONTENTS

PREFACE

One morning several years ago, I received a phone call from Arthur Miller. At the time we were preparing the production of *After the Fall*. It was some two months prior to rehearsal. He said, "It just hit me that this play may be construed as a play about Marilyn." For a moment I was a trifle stunned, and then managed to reply that, of course, we had to face such a probability and that we had always known it. Now, it must be remembered that at this point Mr. Miller had been working consistently on this play for the prior year and a half—consequently, his expression of such a concern at this late hour seemed certainly bewildering, in fact almost obtuse. I was inclined to think, "My God, doesn't the man know what he was writing?" The truth of the matter is that he doesn't always.

This situation was a perfect example of a significant quality that exists in all truly sensitive playwrights. As Mr. Miller points out in the following dialogue with Dr. Richard Evans, "We are bound by a certain unconscious quality." It is this unconscious quality that is finally the heart of the author's talent. *Of course*, a playwright "knows" what he has written on a level quite beyond anyone else, but, deeper than that, he is dealing with a basic emotional life born out of the characters he has conceived and the world in which he is living with them. And on the path down which those characters are taking him (or down which he is taking them—the situation is constantly interchangeable) accidents occur, sometimes inspired accidents. These spontaneous surprises are the very pulse and life of the final work.

It is debatable, though I'm not sure how important the debate is, to what degree the writer is conscious of these immensely significant moments. The technique and mechanics consist, so to speak, in controlling the accident. I think it can be said that this applies to all the arts. The more deeply gifted artist will achieve more accidents and will generally have a greater technique with which to control them.

In the case of Mr. Miller's phone call that morning, I could only feel on consideration that his anxiety, which one might feel should have come a year earlier, actually emerged right on schedule. The fact is, Arthur Miller is an extremely subjective writer (a factor which makes the discussion that follows consistently vital and interesting) and he had spent many months living intimately with the basic emotional life of a play that dealt with a man immobilized (Quentin), seeking through the events and recurring themes of his life a purpose and point to his existence. Now cer-

tainly Mr. Miller was *aware* of the areas in his own
life that he drew upon in creating the design of the
play (particularly in the Maggie-Quentin relationship), *but* his overriding deep emotional concern was
in finally, conclusively, bringing Quentin to an understanding of himself, the unhappy world around him
and his complicity in it—and to enable him, thus
armed, to go forward and attempt to cope with it
again. After many months of literally living inside the
play, Mr. Miller came up for air—took an objective
look at the walls and the windows of the house, so to
speak, and then telephoned me. It was as if he was
saying, "I hope the truth won't be destroyed by the
facts."

I mention this incident because it seems to touch
upon so much of what constitutes the following dialogues—how much the writer's sense of psychological
motivation is conscious and to what extent it sheds
light on him as a human being and an artist. In the
beginning, Dr. Evans observes that "some of the greatest insights into human personality have come, not
from the discipline of psychology, but from the
humanities, art, etc."—that Mr. Miller's plays are "a
superb example of this kind of perceptiveness" and
that "to learn more about your creative psychological
analysis of man, it would be interesting to get your
reactions to some ideas in formal psychological
thought—"

From this point, Dr. Evans embarks on a series of
questions—to which Mr. Miller reacts. At the risk of
sounding like a reviewer, I'd like to say that they both
do what they are supposed to do superbly. Dr. Evans,

psychologist, calmly and penetratingly pursues Mr. Miller, playwright, who calmly and penetratingly refuses, much of the time, to be pursued: "I have read so many attempts to find meaning in plays which are so absurd that it makes me wonder whether there is any value at all in attempts to analyze a writer in terms of his work" or "It's all gossip, psychiatric gossip"—"It's a kind of exercise in futility. I don't know where you get with it or what its purpose is." Finally, Mr. Miller says, "I think one of the reasons we even have this conversation is that culture in terms of the deep and steady use of literature is so sparse in this country. I think in a way psychology is trying to fill a gap. We're creating a psychological culture in the sense that other countries have created a literary or artistic culture." Dr. Evans, undaunted, skillfully pursues his victim with questions and statements, constantly provoking vigorous reactions from Mr. Miller. The upshot is a consistently stimulating conversation which, indeed, reflects the playwright as a human being in what seems to me a thoroughly authentic manner. But, when Mr. Miller says that "we are bound by a certain unconscious quality," Mr. Miller is laying down the ground rules, and though science may be out to penetrate that area, I rather feel that Dr. Evans is aware of the "secret" and around it he effectively builds the conversation toward a continuously realized structure, both in terms of its psychological perspective and in terms of highly interesting, almost "pop" reading.

I remember a marvelous sense of discovery in reading Vasari's *Lives of the Artists*, because the author was able, as a contemporary, to report what happened at breakfast time on a certain day and suddenly Donatello or one of his fellow artists shared with us the commonplace problems of day-to-day existence— it even seemed in some strange way to compel me to gaze a little longer at his work with a sense that I was almost reaching some slight understanding and relationship to it and him. This book may well generate something of this feeling in the reader.

Though the progress of Mr. Miller's daily life is seldom impeded by conventional modesty, he has an immense sense of humility and wonder before the endless surprises and forces of human behavior. He delights in the magnificence of nature, the land and the changing seasons. In fact, he is very conscious of that in his plays. I have spent innumerable sessions with him discussing the quality of the lighting, sounds, or the costumes that might best express the weather, the time of year or the time of day. He is a first-rate carpenter and a second-rate fisherman (we have fished together on a number of occasions). He can also fix a carburetor (a hell of a rare gift among playwrights). I remember once spending a good part of a day with him trying to get my motorcycle started. He has developed a small but fine nursery, and takes great pride in the growth and marketability of his trees. He possesses an almost childlike glee in the discovery of new simple pleasures—this extends to travel, food, a comfortable chair, a brand of tobacco or the latest efficient refrigerator, a new restaurant, homemade bread (among a great many endowments, his wife is a marvelous cook) and, above all, the continual and developing reactions to life of his six-year-old daughter. A functioning home life is of the greatest importance to the atmosphere in which he can work and write productively. He was recently a delegate from Connecticut at the Democratic Convention. Though he returned from the regrettable gathering with a sense of anger and despair, he came bursting into my office and said, "Hey! I sold four more trees!"

Though Arthur Miller, to be sure, embraces the morning sun and the food that follows with a vigorous and innocent gratitude—there is, somehow, a silence within him that seems to be forever watching the light that fails on the distant horizon. It must be remembered that one vision supports the other.

All of us have filed away within us conscious memories of moments in our lives. The degree of their importance varies—at surprising intervals they flash through our mind and sometimes we feel the event remembered is so commonplace and insignificant that we are puzzled as to why we retained that moment at all. This particular characteristic exists in gifted writers to a large degree and to an extraordinary one in the case of Mr. Miller. The slightest quiver in the emotional wave length of the ordinary conversational exchange will register and be immediately impounded in that vast storehouse to be drawn upon by him *at* sometime *in* some way. For most of us it is simply a sentimental remembrance—for him, it is born out of a curious intuitive sense of identification with human need and frailty and it forever haunts him on a remarkable variety of levels—both comic and tragic. I believe its application is almost never consciously psychological. And this brings us back to the "ground rules."

In the many conferences I have had with Arthur, regarding "our" work and the efforts "we" can inject into a production to more fully find its motivation and life, it is as if we are tossing the ball back and forth, but always within the confines of the court. The discussions I hope will continue, but the "ground rules" are there forever—without them, there is no art, for beyond lies the mystery and beauty of the creative act.

Dr. Evans confronts Mr. Miller and together they demonstrate this with immense success. I can only say it has been documented and I am grateful for it.

Robert Whitehead

PSYCHOLOGY
AND
ARTHUR
MILLER

INTRODUCTION

Among the new and important developments in American psychology is one that has been described variously as humanistic, "third force," existential—depending on the focus of the psychologist's orientation. Whatever the orientation, however, these psychologists hold certain important beliefs in common. First, they have a definite commitment to humanistic values. They believe that each man is a unique individual who can and *should* strive for sufficient self-acceptance so that he can truly love his fellowmen. They believe the individual can live in harmony with his fellowmen in society, yet be primarily individualistic or self-determined. The pressures to be shaped completely by social, cultural, environmental, or biological influences can be resisted. Such self-determinism in harmony with society breeds the highest order of individual creativity and productivity. The humanistic view in psychology thus focuses on the

importance of the internal, subjective nature of man
rather than the biological-social-environmental forces
which seemed emphasized in early psychoanalytic or
behaviorist theory. (See Appendix 2 for a more detailed discussion of these trends.)

A challenge to the humanistic psychologist arises
from psychologists who believe that such a commitment cannot be a part of an objective scientific psychology. They, in fact, feel that humanistic values will
lead only to research which is in effect self-fulfilling
prophecy. If the psychologist believes that man is
something in particular, he will keep finding out that
man is something in particular, blinded by his (the
psychologist's) own values.

Many scientific psychologists feel that this type of
value commitment, particularly the emphasis on exis-
tentialism, needlessly clutters the psychologist's en-
deavors. Granted that if the psychologist seeks to
understand the individual, all sorts of speculations
might be interesting—humanistic, existential, or whatever—but this isn't the true goal of a psychological
science. The true goal should be to predict and control behavior. Prediction and control of man's behavior
can be effected by environmental manipulation, without necessarily understanding man.

Within the context of these divergent views in contemporary psychology lies the fascination of Arthur
Miller. For Miller in my opinion more than any contemporary playwright not only comes to grips with
this issue, but comes to grips with it in a profoundly
brilliant manner. In fact, throughout the history of
man, creative thinkers in the humanities have pre-

sented the strongest case for the very humanistic values to which the "third force" group of psychologists adhere.

I was thus delighted when Miller agreed to participate in our National Science Foundation project which has included films and a series of books based on dialogues with such psychologists as Carl Jung, Ernest Jones, Erich Fromm, Erik Erikson, B. F. Skinner, Raymond Cattell, Nevitt Sanford, Ernest Hilgard, Henry Murray, Gardner Murphy, and Gordon Allport. (See Appendix 1 for a detailed discussion of the rationale for this project.)

The problem of how to develop a productive confrontation between a psychologist and a playwright, who, as the reader will note in the text of the dialogue, is not exactly a strong supporter of many of the values he perceives in contemporary psychology, presented a fascinating challenge. One way has been to provide an opportunity for Miller to express his views of how he, as a creative writer, develops his characterizations in his plays, and explore with him the "theories" of personality that he applied in this process. Also explored is Miller's approach in developing motives in his characters and what he has in mind from the standpoint of the desired impact on the audience.

Another area of discussion deals with Miller's direct reactions to some of the existing formal concepts in personality psychology which, at least superficially, would seem to have some relationship to the process of characterization in a play. (See Recommended Readings for a list of references relating to this facet of the discussion.) Miller reacts to the trait theory of

Gordon Allport, role theory, the feelings of inferiority notion of Alfred Adler, Kurt Lewin's field theory, Carl Jung's notion of archetypes, and Freudian unconscious symbolism. It is apparent that such formalized psychological concepts often fail to make much sense to him, and he expresses this in no uncertain terms. Elsewhere, Miller is given the opportunity to relate the content of his work to contemporary society and social psychology.

The result of this confrontation between psychologist and writer hopefully avoids some of the pitfalls of similarly recorded discussions of the past. For example, I have deliberately avoided dwelling on Miller's own personality for its own sake and instead provided an opportunity for him to discuss his approach to personality as reflected in his work. At the same time I also believe that as I explore with Miller his style of creativity or how he develops characters in his plays, more significant things about Miller the man are revealed than might be the case through some kind of pseudo-analytical interview which might have attempted to reveal Miller the man more directly. In fact, in examining the content of most of the interviews completed so far with the highly creative individuals participating in this project, I have concluded that as a creative individual discusses his own most cherished ideas and work, he reveals much of himself as a person in the process.

One of the most disturbing trends in criticism of contemporary drama and literature is the misapplication of psychological generalizations. Some critics will use their personal, and often limited, perceptions of the playwright's own personality and background to attempt to determine the "real" meaning of the play. For example, in response to Arthur Miller's most recent play, *The Price*, some critics pointed out that they felt that the play reflected Miller's Depression philosophy or the struggles in Miller's own family. In fact, one of the things that was particularly interesting to me in my discussion with Miller was on this very point. He contends that such generalizations about the work of a writer are in the final analysis irrelevant. I might add that such a focus in terms of the psychology of projection may tell more about the critic—his biases and prejudices—than about the playwright or play itself. However, I hope that aside from revealing something of Miller and his creative process, some significant insights about creativity as a psychological process in general emerge.

Although my questions or remarks were not intended primarily to be critical, Mr. Miller was exceedingly forthright in his responses when, in the "devil's advocate" role, I occasionally presented questions challenging some of his conceptions and responded to some of his statements by clarifying what I felt were his misconceptions of psychology.

As was the case with subjects of the earlier books in the series (Jung, Fromm, Erikson, Skinner), it is hoped that the discussion format allows the reader to be introduced to or to reexamine some of Mr. Miller's ideas in a somewhat different framework. In his own writing, Miller has the opportunity to rewrite and to polish until he deems the finished product satisfactory. In our discussion, however, he was called upon to develop his ideas extemporaneously. I hope that this element of spontaneity assists in penetrating to the "man behind the playwright" while losing none of the ideas central to Miller's unique creative process. Because preservation of this naturalness of communication is essential to the purposes of each volume in this series, few liberties have been taken with the basic content of Miller's responses to my questions, although some editorial license had to be exercised to shift effectively from oral to printed communication, in the service of accuracy, readability, clarity, and grammatical construction. In fact, Miller was given the opportunity later to edit and expand answers to some of my questions.

So this dialogue as it is presented here duplicates insofar as possible the tenor of the exchange between Mr. Miller and myself as it actually took place. In spite of some of the editing which was necessary in both Miller's responses, as indicated above, and my questions, it was a pleasant surprise to review our hours of discussion content and see how few deletions and alterations were required. The flow of material, though extemporaneous, is sufficiently well organized to be of interest to students of drama, literature or psychology, as well as to the general reader who shares my fascination with Mr. Miller's considerable contribution to our culture. I particularly hope this dialogue makes available some reactions not readily obtainable from the more traditional discussion of Miller and his work.

I would like to reiterate that the questions presented to Mr. Miller are designed to allow his views to emerge as coherently yet as spontaneously as possible. This was a situation far from ideal for him to be expected to produce a polished presentation of his ideas, yet, as pointed out earlier, he was obviously able to organize his thoughts in a most communicative manner. Thus, an essentially integrated presentation has resulted from this confrontation between a psychologist and a powerful writer.

THE WRITER AS CREATOR

PART I

EVANS: Mr. Miller, there is no doubt that some of the greatest insights into human personality have come not from the discipline of psychology, but from the humanities—art, literature, drama. Many of us would regard your insights concerning man in your many plays as a superb example of this kind of perceptiveness by creative writers. To learn more about your creative psychological analysis of man, it would be interesting to get your reactions to some ideas in formal psychological thought which might at least be superficially relevant to your construction of a play, its characterizations, themes, and its impact on the audience. To begin our discussion in this vein, I might mention that one of the things that is particularly apparent in your work is your sophistication concerning the psychology of motivation, which includes the needs that arouse, direct, and sustain the individual. In order to understand a person, we must try to understand something about these needs. Such understanding requires us first to be able to distinguish between mask and substance; that is, one can observe the facade or mask of an individual but to really understand his personality, one must deal with substance and look at the "dynamics" which underlie his behavior. Does this distinction, between mask and substance, make any sense to you? As you develop characterization in your plays, do you look at it from this vantage point?

MILLER: Of course, that is the basis of any story. Overtly or by implication in any drama the writer sets up what seems normal or what seems to be in equilibrium in the beginning of the work and then shows what the inner contradictions are in that situation or personality, so that the idea of mask and substance, as you call it, is a given quantity. As you know, the original Greek drama was performed with masks for a very good reason; the mask represented the symbolic or overt function, while the action developed the internal conflict and perhaps revealed the subjective truth behind the mask. You know, it is a device that many modern writers have used directly, but any story, any drama, does inevitably involve that tension between the symbolic and individual functions of man.

EVANS: It seems to me that in your plays you have used both symbolic and psychological forms for a variety of reasons. For example, in *Death of a Salesman*, you give an amazingly complete picture of the motivations of your characters. In *The Crucible*, however, motivation may be important but the characters seem to be prototypes—symbols of the individual's reaction against society. Does this type of analysis seem valid to you?

MILLER: Well, a difference in intention creates difference in form. *The Crucible* is involved essentially with the social relations of human beings, and consequently, the predominant emphasis in writing the play was on the conflict between people rather than the conflict within somebody. In *Death of a Salesman*, the emphasis is more subjective, principally, I suppose, because what I was interested in there was what Willy's world and his life had done to his personality and how he was struggling with the total experience that he had lived through. As a matter of fact, the title that I started with was *The Inside of His Head*, and at one time I thought of having a vast proscenium with a face that opened and the whole play taking place inside his skull. It's a matter of emphasis; you can do certain things better with one approach than you can with another. *The Crucible* is in a more epic form; the individual is seen through society. The other is in a more realistic or psychological form; society is seen through the individual.

EVANS: Of course, there is a parallel in society itself; that is, we might look at a conspicuous public figure, and we don't really know the substance, the personality organization of this man. We simply know him because he is opposed to something or in favor of something, and of course, we get to know him as a person when we begin to understand his motives. In a sense, this raises the question of the degree to which perhaps even in life we categorize our relationships. We sometimes relate to certain people only in terms of the mask, whereas we relate to others in terms of substance. Now, when you depict these two orientations, do you feel that you are depicting people as

they are in life, that perhaps we see people as mask
or substance or perhaps both?

MILLER: That's a dangerous idea, "as they are in
life," because it is really as my sensibility translates
life. A writer records facts in order to transcend them,
to unearth their inner coherency. The means of doing
this are his style and his style is an expression of his
personality. That's a different emphasis entirely. We
don't want personality in a newspaper reporter or
even, to a certain extent, in a scientist. Without personality, without the subjective reflection of events, it
is impossible to conceive of a creative writer. So what
we are asking for, and what one tries to do, I think, is
to say in effect that as the writer, I am almost as important as what I am registering, that I am a part of
this moment and the play is what the moment has
been to me. Now, I happen to believe that more often
than not, the stamp of the times will be found in the
literature rather than in any other field. That's a tricky
question and a very complicated one, but I think that
in the past you would look toward the arts to find out
what the spirit of the people was, what the total picture might have been, not just politics, fashions, or
manners, but some sort of totality could best be gath-
ered from literature because that is the way the artist
registers it, as a total, as a whole. "Life as it is" is
fragmentary.

EVANS: To discuss your characterizations a bit further, as I view your plays, something rather interesting
occurs. I find that by the time you have completed
your analysis, description, and presentation of the characters you develop, very few of them are people that

one would dislike. Even those who have committed crimes against society, such as Joe Keller in *All My Sons*, or who have committed crimes of morality, such as Willy Loman in *Death of a Salesman*, emerge as sympathetic characters. This phenomenon is interesting to me because many psychologists have suggested that if we can examine the underlying motives of other people, most of our stereotypes, our negative feelings, and our hatreds will dissolve. Now, does this kind of judgment about your work make any sense; that is, would you also say that most of your characters were not hated by the audience?

MILLER: I would say at most times they're not, but I'm glad if that means my characters are seen from their own viewpoints. I don't think you could understand anybody—and in a sense it equates with the open-mindedness of good science—without a tremendous amount of empathy or putting yourself in the position of that person. If you are disposed to be disgusted at some physiological process, you can't very well enter into an investigation of it. You would be blind; your disgust or your hatred would keep you from seeing whole parts of it. So that in a way the drama is there, at least I hope mine is, in order to suggest a deeper perception of the world in terms of sharing the points of view of other people. No one could write a good play unless he were able to shift his point of view every time he writes a line. It's a constant shifting of empathy; I'm with one man at one moment and then I have to go right over to the other side and be with the other man for a moment. The truth of the whole play depends exactly upon that ability to jump into the skin of the opposing party in the conflict, and consequently, if you mean that they are acceptable to you in the sense that they seem justified, that their nature seems justified, well, that's the way it ought to be. Any other way, they're just drawn from stencils.

EVANS: Essentially what we're saying is that in the development of a character, it's a good deal more difficult to try to create the motives which will elicit a unique empathy than to merely present stereotyped characterizations for which the audience reaction is "ready-made."

MILLER: Well, it's the only difficulty, finally. A lot of people can tell a story, but the autonomy of its characters goes beyond, and I think, reflects just that, the empathic ability. We think Shakespeare is so universal for one reason, and that is that he obviously could share the inner life of a variety of personalities to such a degree that he himself has rather vanished into his plays.

EVANS: Now, to move to a slightly different focus. One of the most difficult problems in the psychologist's study of personality is that he is really studying himself. There is always the calculated risk that the dynamics of his own personality will interfere and distort what he believes to be objective observations. As much as he tries to be scientifically detached, he may be guilty of distortion in his findings. For example, one frequent observation that has been made about Freud is that the preoccupation in psychoanalysis with the Oedipus conflict resulting from the male child falling in love with the mother and hating the father, was really a reflection of the fact that his own father was many years older than his mother and he may have had this very Oedipal conflict himself. In other words, in his writing Freud was really acting out a personal conflict. In a sense the writer in literature and drama may even be more subject to such criticism than Freud. As the writer, for example, develops certain characters and conflicts in his novels or plays, how can he avoid reflecting his own personality dynamics? How do you feel about this? Is it important to consider whether or not the personality, background, and experience of the writer should be separated from his creative effort? Should we read into his creative effort whatever we can learn about the writer as a human being, or should we just look at the product as it stands alone?

MILLER: It's a lot of fun to choose the first method, but I have read so many attempts to find meaning in my plays which are so absurd that it makes me wonder whether there is any value at all in the attempts to analyze a writer in terms of his work. There is to a degree, of course. It's obvious that you can do that, but in any subtle, fine way I think it is really impossible. The analyzer, after all, is projecting his own personality into his analysis. The writer is not all that simple, not more than any other individual is, and these so to speak remnants of his personality that might be usable in his play could be elements that are only partially descriptive of his nature. There are exceptions. There are lyric novelists like Thomas Wolfe, for instance, whom one could read and guess a great deal about his personality through his work, but I think that it is a rare work that one could analyze truthfully and say anything conclusive about the writer. There's too much contradictory evidence. When I did *Salesman*, they were convinced that the oldest son represented me, and then it was the boy next door, and then it was the youngest son, and then it was Willy himself. Some people said it was the mother. Well, they all made good cases for each theory, so much so that they all cancelled out. I think what a writer does in effect is to partition himself if the work is of any use. If it's good as a play, he portions himself out among the various characters, if you want to look at it that way at all. To the degree that he can sympathize with them, he has identified with them, but they have their own complexity which really begins where the writer's left off. There is, in other words, such a thing as a work of art which is imaginary. It flows from the inner dynamics of a situation and creates wholly new traits, even in the author, so that he is sometimes changed by the fact that he's written something. There is a dialectic involved which is extraordinarily complicated. He can take on what seems like a new personality, even from having gone through the writing of a work, so that any one-to-one identification in the work is impossible, I think. It leaves out the whole idea of imagination and the whole idea of creation. Confession may be the beginning of art but never its end.

EVANS: Then you would not consider it particularly important to worry about Freud's personal life or to make some guesses about it. You'd study what he contributed on its own merits.

MILLER: I can't see the ultimate importance of Freud's personal life, no. I think that it is probably not as interesting as the personal lives of people who are much less important to the world. In other words, his importance to the world is not that he had a father who was much older than his mother. It's the fact that he was a great creative mind that is of interest and that he created certain vital conceptions, and I think that is harder to understand. Let me say this: I think there's an escape hatch for literary critics as well as others in getting too involved in trying to see the author in his work, the escape hatch from the work itself, from deciding what one really feels about it, what one has gotten out of it, whether it's alive or dead. It's much easier to sit there and say, "Well, obviously this man has an unresolved Oedipal situation, and his grandmother dropped him on his head when he was nine years old." Well, what do you know when you know that? Absolutely nothing. It's all gossip, psychiatric gossip.

EVANS: Of course, this is something that Freud himself is guilty of in a way, in his analysis of da Vinci.

MILLER: Yes, he set the stage for this kind of analysis to some degree. Of course, I don't think Freud himself was necessarily claiming that this was anything but an interesting foray in the analysis of an artist through his work. As I recall, he made that analysis of da Vinci in order to demonstrate a point. It was not just to find out what da Vinci was like, but how certain principles operated. Now what you were talking about is, as I say, just gossip. It's a kind of

exercise in "nothing-but-ism," a depreciation of art itself. I don't know where you get with it or what its
purpose is except to supplant the art work with
analytic material. I'm sure it's hard enough to analyze
somebody who's lying right there on a couch and who
presumably is making his inner life more or less available. Well, how are you going to analyze someone by
trying to get through the screen of what very often is
a defensive mechanism, like a work of art? I mean a
man might write a book in order to convince himself
of exactly the opposite of what is true about him, and
he might get away with it. Artists are forever trying
to become their opposites. You see, he might be exer-
cising a previously nonexistent sense of power by writing that work of art, and you might very well get
taken in if he's a good enough artist.

EVANS: Your point about da Vinci is a good one.
Freud's analysis was really an exercise to study the
scope of what could be done with the technique, and
I think that this fact is often misunderstood. But to
get back to the other points, we have discussed the
writer and his personality and its bearing on his work,
and we've talked about the characters in a drama and
how we might interpret them. We can also look at a
play through the naïve interpretations of the audience.
In this respect, there is a whole body of literature in
psychology dealing with what is sometimes called
"selective perception." It argues that there is not a
simple one-to-one relationship between "reality" and
man's perception of it; that man's perception involves
a complicated, often distorting, selective, filtering
process of the real world about him. The more vague

or ambiguous a stimulus is (e.g., an ink blot) the more likely is the perception of it reflective of the needs, attitudes or values of the perceiver. Of course, works of art such as plays in a sense become almost like massive ink blot tests, where the interpretations by the members of the audience may sometimes reveal more about themselves than any pervasive truths about the play itself or for that matter the playwright. An example of the process of audience "selective perception" is the reaction to *Death of a Salesman*. There appears to be a kind of "open-endedness" about it, the sense that you were not trying to structure it too highly for the audience. Correct me if I'm wrong, but you appear to be deliberately allowing an effect to emerge which approaches a stream of consciousness. You didn't appear to articulate its precise meaning too fully. Was that effect created because you wanted to be sure that the impact of this play on the audience allows for a certain amount of "selective perception"?

MILLER: I would not put it just that way. Rather, I'd say that *Death of a Salesman* is a highly structured work in this sense: I developed the form in order to obviate the necessity of having to say things that are not of the first importance, so that the play is extremely selective. What seems to be a stream of consciousness is quite the opposite. It is actually a mosaic of pieces, each one of which begins where its thematic importance begins and not before, and ends where its thematic importance is finished. That is what gives you the impressionistic effect. In life, or in plays that try to seem like life, a lot of ineffectual dialogue occurs, introductions and people just mumbling on and on about nothing at all in order to get to a point where naturalistically, they could say what the playwright has in his head to say. I leaped all that, so that there is a high degree of selectivity in the play, and perhaps that is what gives it the feeling that you mentioned. In other words, I'm trying to make the point that the dialogue is not a glob of undifferentiated material. It may appear that way, thank God. I mean one is not aware that in fact *Salesman* is probably my most densely structured play, that the material is so strictly selected that it is always connected thematically. Not necessarily in terms of the words themselves, but by the unexpected centrality of diverse ideas.

EVANS: You've made a very interesting distinction between the craftsmanship involved in a play's structure and, in a sense, the impact of the play as a whole. You seem to be pleased that as a whole it has this kind of broad impressionistic effect and that to some degree, something is left up to the member of the audience to judge and evaluate. Is this a desirable end, then, as you see it?

MILLER: I don't want you to imagine that one sits down and says, "Now, I want to create this effect, and therefore, I will go about it this way." Quite the contrary, the ultimate effect is something you can't imagine. I can't; all I can do is express a vision which I suppose is modified in part by my subconscious sense of how to touch people, or how to move them, how to reach them. So that is part of the vision, too, I suppose, but my confidence is that what moves me deeply will move somebody else. I'm not always right. If I'm moved to laughter when I'm writing, very often people are moved to tears at that very moment, but I'm not laughing at something, I'm laughing with joy, perhaps, that I have discovered this. You see, there is some inner irony that's so complete that even though it's tragic, I might be laughing because a whole is forming, something alive. That doesn't mean I'm out of sympathy with the character at all; it simply means that effects are the end result of something that one can't predict, especially in the theater.

EVANS: Selective distortion of a play's meaning might involve the professional critic as well as any other member of the audience, might it not?

MILLER: I'll give you objective examples. *The Crucible* was produced in 1953 in an atmosphere of McCarthyism and all the rest. The critics, who despite themselves had imbibed the atmosphere of the times even though they might not have been sympathetic to McCarthyism, were filled with suspicions and what I believe to be a paranoia from which we are still suffering. I mean paranoia in the real medical sense of the word, not as a literary metaphor. The critics regarded it as a cold play. Well, it ran about six or seven months and then was played all over the world and then was played again in New York, the same play exactly. The new production was about five or six years later, and to make a long story shorter, the same reviewers, more or less, found it to be a really burning hot play to the degree that one of them took it upon himself to say that I had changed the play. We had improved the production, but of course the same exact script was used in both productions.

EVANS: So as I suggested earlier, it would seem
that the viewer of a play often reacts selectively to the
things that are perhaps more reflective of the "dynamics" of his own personality rather than those of
the playwright's.

MILLER: Yes. But I'm not sure I object to all that.
I think that part of the function of any art is to be an
arena of suggestion for the onlooker. It's to open him
up to himself and cause his psyche to unwind and to
be stimulated. Beyond certain very narrow limits, I
don't think you can predict or control people's reactions; on the contrary, I would like to release their
reactions, provided certain very minimal objective elements of communication in the play are received.
Beyond that, they are on their own. I can't argue with
that; I think it's a good thing.

EVANS: To pursue this point further, in the interpretation of writing, there is one extreme view of this
process that might be called "phenomenological." For
example, no "universal meaning" can be ascribed to a
certain type of poem because its only "meaning," if
any, is simply what each reader naïvely believes it to
be from the standpoint of his subjective impression of
it. The poetry of Dylan Thomas might be described
in this manner. The extreme opposite of this "phenomenological" style would be a "formula" type of
writing, where virtually every intended effect on the
reader is spelled out in detail. For example, in certain
pulp fiction or television drama, interpretations are
literally handed to the audience. In a sense, you are
describing your work as something between these
extremes, is that correct?

MILLER: Yes, I'd say so. I think the rhapsodic nature of lyric poetry makes it awkward to descend to any literal or prescribed meaning such as you could with plays, including lyric plays, which are much more structured in terms of communicating something than a lyric poem. It's a bit like the difference between a song and speech. The elements that are most important to the appreciation of a song are the suggestive, the musical ones. The same thing is true, I think, of lyric poetry.

EVANS: To review our discussion so far, we have dealt with personality psychology from the standpoint of mask, substance, and motivation as a framework in which to examine various views of a play. We have looked at a play from the standpoint of its characters and their motives, the playwright and his motives, and we have just discussed how the motives of the person watching the play may enter into his interpretation of it—how he may "selectively perceive" it. Perhaps we could now explore further some of the implications of these three views of a play. Some psychological truisms which might afford additional perspective on this are: in some ways, all people are alike; in some ways, some people are like some other people; and in some ways, each person is different from every other person. Now, if we talk about certain universal motives which you bring into your drama which reflect the ways in which people are all alike, we are discussing those things that the entire audience can identify with most easily. I guess this is why so many writers deal in universal motives like sex. The ways in which some people are like some other people

present a distinction which can also offer some audience identification. For example, striving for achievement, as an example of such a motive, will be responded to by many members of the audience. However, when you attempt to portray the uniqueness of
a character, the ways in which he differs from every
other person, how do you elicit audience comprehension? This uniqueness of a character would seem to
be the most difficult thing to communicate. Of course,
this kind of breakdown might seem artificial to a creative writer, but would it make any sense to you to
think in these terms about characterization and the
effects of the characters on the audience?

MILLER: I don't think in those terms, but I suppose the way I operate could be abstracted into those
terms, perhaps. I think anybody who writes is trying
to communicate something. It may be a negative communication, in the sense that he really feels better if
fewer people understand him, and he's not striving to
hold a large number of people. In the theater, at least
the theater that I was brought up in, the nature of
the beast is such that the play is a dynamic operation.
One can't stop a play and say, "Well, I didn't quite
understand what was meant there. Now go back and
read that over again." There must be a certain minimal
communication at every single moment of a play, of
the acting out of it, so that people are not completely
at sea in the course of the thing. That means that you
are operating on the basis, I suppose, that the writer
has a grasp of what most people are like, and he as-
sumes that most people are like most other people.
Each of my plays deals with an extreme conflict in

an ordinary person. To tell the truth, I don't regard
my characters as persons in the way you are thinking.
They're images and effects on me, the hidden and
veiled reactions to the world. You see, I don't think
you can look at dramatic characters the way you look
at people. They aren't really individuals. They are a
set of conflicting relationships on the stage. I don't
know very much about Oedipus; no one does. You
know those elements in him which are in the fore-
front of his reaction to a particular situation. But is
Oedipus a good father or a bad father? Is he greedy,
or is he generous? You know, all the usual character-
istics of human beings don't even apply. You don't
even ask these questions. The author really puts before the audience a certain limited group of questions
to which he is prepared to give responses in the
course of the action. It is hoped that through the intense answers that one gives, an imaginary fullness
can be conveyed. I think it's a two-way street; that is,
the play does so much, and the audience does the
rest. You reach sensitivities in the audience, some of
them bizarre. I have to add again that this is not part
of the creative apparatus, and I don't think about
these things while writing. As we talk I am rational-
izing after the fact. I wouldn't know how to solve
these problems as problems in psychology. But I think
it's an error to look at characters in literature the way
one looks at real people. There is something missing.
At best the dramatic character is a vivid dialectical
impression. By "dialectical" I mean that when he does
one thing, there is a response which in turn creates a
a counterforce. What I'm dealing with are these con-

stant reverberations. It's rather like physics, I suppose.
Every action has a reaction, and there is something
wrong about equating these forces with real people.
Ibsen once wrote a play—I believe it was *Hedda
Gabler*—and in the manuscript he referred to her as,
I think, forty-seven years of age. A perceptive friend
watched the performance, and afterward he said that
the woman couldn't possibly be forty-seven. Her
father died at a given age, and the mathematics simply wouldn't work out. She couldn't possibly be over
thirty years of age. Ibsen stoutly denied it and was
very insulted because he was a very careful craftsman,
and that anybody would question his knowledge of his
own characters was to him an insult. But two days
later he wrote the friend a letter and he said, "You
know, you are perfectly right." The interesting thing
about it is that in thinking of this woman in her forties,
he had made a dreadful error. A woman in her forties
is a slightly different person from a woman in her
early thirties, but his objective mind had told him
that she was forty-seven years of age, and that's the
age he gave her. But inside him somewhere, the truth
was being told—she was behaving like a woman of
thirty. Now he was doing something he didn't even
know he was doing, and I think that is the essence of
the matter. To objectify these things too far is very
difficult, like resolving to be wise.

EVANS: So you feel that the psychologist's way of
pointing to the uniqueness of the individual would
require the playwright to be too objective or precise.
In fact, you seem to feel that this general approach to
analyzing the personality of the individual may not

be too helpful to the playwright as he develops his characterizations and hopefully elicits audience identification.

MILLER: I would mention here the essence of the matter, and that is feeling. What you are really identifying with is an intensity of feeling that is reasonably clear. A writer has an intense feeling. It supersedes everything else. Without that there is no work of art, there is no theater, there is nothing. And what the audience is doing basically is reacting to my feeling. They are accepting it or rejecting it or sharing it or refusing to share it. And that process is further complicated by the time and place and culture in which the audience is situated. As I said, with *The Crucible*, the same play in the same country five years later was a different play. In one production it seemed cold as ice and the next time it was as hot as a firecracker. Nothing had changed, but the time had changed; the relationship of people to their government, the world, the crises in Berlin, and the rest of the whole business had created what you'd say were different people. Their feelings were now allowed to sympathize with somebody caught in a witch hunt. And in McCarthy's time they couldn't afford to feel that. So, you're dealing with dynamics that are very fluid. Now to come back to your earlier question, it's impossible therefore ever to think of writing something in terms of what the audience is going to make out of it. I don't know. I've started a play and sometimes it takes a year or two to write it. How do I know what's going to happen two years hence? It could be a very different country. I must therefore deal with certain fundamentals, what seem to me to be relatively timeless dilemmas inside people.

EVANS: To pursue this point about the impact on the audience a little further, we might discuss the ways in which a play may contribute to the growth of the audience. In your plays, you are admittedly not talking about real people, yet the focus of your characterization is such that it allows a particular kind of identification by at least some members of the audience and may lead to some psychological growth. This growth might involve a keener insight into themselves or others. Another possibility might be growth in an ideological sense. You may have been able to persuade —to perhaps change a point of view. Of course, historically we have examples of many plays that have done this with respect to vital issues of the day. Another effect of a play might be to simply provide entertainment for the audience. Perhaps the playwright can combine all these things in a single effort —affect the personality and ideology of the audience in the process of entertaining. What satisfies you the most as you become aware of the impact of one of your plays? What are the things that make you feel the happiest?

MILLER: I think the feeling or the knowledge that I brought news from nowhere to people, either some insight about themselves (which is generally the case, when something comes off, that is) or insight about the world, about others. I think that when you speak of growth and the possibility of growth in relation to drama, and I believe that drama is important to such things and so are art and literature, I'd put it this way:

most of us have one great difficulty in life, and that is to see ourselves as others see us and to see the other person as he sees himself. Without that second process, seeing him as he sees himself, not only is sympathy impossible but understanding is also impossible. And if the drama is a real one, your allegiance to one character is constantly being tested, is being broken off and challenged at every single step of the way. So it isn't a question of being right or wrong but of his perception of reality being correct or incorrect, because at one point Hamlet, for example, is merely suspicious, at the next moment he's certain, and pretty soon you see that the issue is not so much whether or not he is certain but that he must act with whatever knowledge he does have. And you become challenged yourself because then you are seeing his point of view, and the point of view of those around him plus your own. That stretching of one's viewpoint toward oneself and the world and the fragmentation of it sometimes and the final healing of it all into a new synthesis is the process of growth, in my opinion. People who don't grow are people who never can enter a world which is not comfortably their own.

EVANS: Unfortunately, very little is known in a systematic clinical or scientific sense about the nature of the impact of a drama as it's actually performed in a theater on the individual members of the audience. However, one psychiatrist, Jacob L. Moreno, has investigated the use of role playing in a clinical setting —or as he calls it, "psychodrama"—as a means of contributing to such growth. The therapeutic value of this technique would stem from the same thesis that you are developing, that the drama can contribute to emotional growth by helping us gain a deeper insight into ourselves and others. However, how do we know if this has happened? How do we make a distinction between an experience, that although gripping for the moment, just passes and an experience that effects a genuine change in the personality of the members of the audience?

MILLER: I don't know how to answer that. I think it's extremely difficult for people to change by virtue of any one incident. In fact, it's probably impossible. If there is anything that causes some change in a person, it is an accretion of experiences—more exactly, a repetition of conflicts, which finally seem to total up to some kind of a new truth for him. I'm speaking of emotional change now. He comes to see the fruitlessness of certain repetitive conflicts. I wouldn't know how to measure that or even how to begin to describe it. That's the psychologist's job.

EVANS: Yes, of course, but rigorous evaluation of the long-term effects of any particular experience on a person's personality is very difficult to accomplish. However, we have to assume that many experiences in life, aside from formal psychotherapy, contribute to emotional growth. For that reason, your observation concerning drama is very interesting. You apparently do believe that some emotional growth can indeed result from viewing a significant drama.

MILLER: I know it does happen. But, strictly speaking, I'm not interested in making people grow in the sense that I want to cure them of anything. Quite honestly I don't think I am motivated to do that if you are interested in it from that point of view. One gets obsessed by certain images of reality, and there is a certain beauty in putting them down within an esthetic form that can reach catharsis, and that's the process. What happens to the audience as a result of the play is of another order. That is to say, I'm not blind to the effects on the audience, and I don't think they're unimportant, but there's literally nothing I can do about them. I've got enough to do to try to write these things. I suppose that earlier on in life I had illusions that one could change the world with a certain kind of drama. Then I lost those illusions altogether, and now I'm in the process of believing that maybe men do live by images more than one suspected before, that despite themselves, and unknowingly, they behave according to some artistic or esthetic ideas which they are not even aware they have digested. There are many instances where art as art creates a fashion—for example, in women's clothing. Mondrian makes a drawing which was certainly not designed to change women's fashions, and suddenly twenty-five years later, they're designing clothes to look like the drawing. Picasso's designs have crept into modern hotel design, and they have changed the idea of what people think of as modern or up-to-date or corny. All art has its effect, but since it's unpredictable, it's not part of my business to dwell on it too long. I want to tell them the truth as I see it, and I think inevitably they are stretched and anguished and perhaps come to share a certain kind of suffering which their lives would never make them conscious of. And out of suffering sometimes comes a little wisdom, but it's all very uncertain. The pre-Hitler Germans were the greatest lovers of good theater in the world.

EVANS: One would be tempted to try to determine whether your work has become less idealistic or more idealistic as the years have gone by.

MILLER: It's no less idealistic, but it is less morally apocalyptic. I think it's more realistic now. I think people change extremely slowly and through a process of accretion if I'm any guide. I know that I'm that way, and most of the people I know are that way. To think that a work of art is going to overthrow igno-rance, for example, or the absence of charity or some-thing else, that's a pretty impossible dream. But it can help unveil reality, the present in history, and that is very important.

EVANS: Incidentally, relating back to our discus-sion of the motivations of your characters and the im-pact on the audience, it would be interesting to have some specific examples of reactions to some of your plays. For example, how did the audience react to Willy Loman in *Death of a Salesman*?

MILLER: Well, there were some people who felt that he was just a failure, he was a fool, but one guy told me that had he joined a union, he'd have been all right. Some other people felt that he was simply an inefficient, stupid fellow, and that's why he got in trouble. There are always people whose minds stop at the literal situation—some critics among them. But I think the majority understood quite well that involved here was the naked individual confronting the pre-cepts of the society. They can't always verbalize it that way, but if the letters I get are any guide they know that a generalization is at work here, more than merely a single case, more even than the question of Willy's personality. It may be worth mentioning, though, that the people who are having a real and active problem with their fathers, sons, mothers, wives, identify themselves with Biff or Linda as much as with Willy. The women especially see it as basically the story of Linda's troubles with this kind of husband. The young people see it as the story of Biff's problems with this kind of a parent. I have had many letters— I still get them—telling how after seeing the play they found a perspective on their own relations with others, and I suppose it gave them some strength to face their lives a little better. This kind of growth does happen, how often I can't say. But surely certain people live as much by the artistic images they receive as they do by their own personal experience. A play can, so to speak, tell them what to make of what they've lived through. But you can only put into people what will pass through the grids in front of their minds. We reject what won't go through, that's all.

EVANS: Speaking of the writer's goals concerning the effects of his play on the audience, I think we have some plays currently on Broadway whose authors might have been motivated simply to get out something that would sell quickly, having been overwhelmed with the desperation of not being able to sell anything, much less something directed toward a profound impact on the audience. In many fields of endeavor, there is often a certain point in a man's career when he can have the luxury of not having to worry about selling something, but this may not be true in your field because of the very importance of the reaction of an audience.

MILLER: Yes, it's always true.

EVANS: Pursuing further this matter of audience reaction, do you usually have a preconceived notion of the composition of the audience to whom you are directing a play, or do you just seek some sort of general impact of a play on a diverse audience?

MILLER: I think that even as the same writer grows older—I hesitate to say matures—the goals change, and the attitudes toward the audience change. When I started, the audience consisted simply of a body of people who would confirm what for me was only theoretical but which I wanted to believe, and that was that I could write good plays. So that what was involved was self-proof. This isn't all that was involved, but it played a large part in creating anything. And I spoke of uniqueness before, that this is what I was. The idea of what I was preceded what I was, obviously. It had gone back years, and that authenticating element is strong. The audience acted as a corroborator. Then the point comes where you see that apparently you can do this, so that the element of the corroborator becomes less vital, although it never disappears, and the content of what you're doing becomes more important, even though the content may appear to be equally important or unimportant from one play to another. My attitude toward it has changed, and I think this is true of a lot of writers. Some of them quit after a little while because once they've proven themselves, that's all they're really interested in. In short, the work itself, its intrinsic value, becomes the overwhelming important thing.

EVANS: Speaking of your intended audience, I ran across a little booklet you wrote, entitled *Jane's Blanket*, a children's book. I let my little daughter read it and she smiled as she expressed a certain pleasurable reaction to the story's charm. However, perhaps you were trying to do more than provide children with a pleasurable reaction. Were you trying to communicate the idea that as a child grows up, he must learn to give up certain things that were important when he was younger?

MILLER: You see now, this is the difference between one way of looking at it and another. My daughter's name is Jane, my eldest daughter, and it was written to her. She's now twenty-one years old. A friend, Louis Untermeyer, came one day, and said, "You must write a children's book because I have a contract to supply six children's books!" I wasn't doing anything, and I said, "Well, if I can do it in half an hour, I'll do it." And I knew this story; I knew the basis of it, which had always moved me because my daughter Jane used to do the same thing. She was stuck on a blanket the way a lot of children are, and it would drive me nuts because we'd go off somewhere, and I'd be halfway there and suddenly she'd raise hell because the blanket wasn't there. I'd have to go all the way back and get it or there'd be no peace. So there was the memory of the pathos of passing through this moment when the security object or the fetish or whatever it is disappears. The loss of one's babyhood was really what was involved in the

story. Now I wouldn't deny the lesson that it taught
in terms of the maturation of a child, but it wasn't of
the first importance to me. It was the emotional quality of the experience that was of interest to me, perhaps a memory I wanted to catch.

EVANS: This really gets back to one of your earlier
comments when we were discussing audience identification with a play's characters. Perhaps we can pursue this interesting point further using *Death of a
Salesman* as an example. It would seem to me that
aside from words and ideas and language and perhaps
symbols, *Salesman* communicates a *total* effect, and it
is this effect that makes the play truly a masterpiece.
How do you seek this? Do you consciously believe
that there is some emotional effect that is communi-
cated and transcends the action, the words, the
symbols?

MILLER: Absolutely. As a matter of fact, if all the
words are there and all the symbols and that effect
isn't there, you've got nothing. Speaking now purely
from the writer's point of view, I think what it comes
down to is that there are certain moments when you
conceive something, some situation or person, which
has life; that is, by some means that I don't know how
to trace and I'm not sure I'd really want to trace it,
you find yourself standing in the center of that person
or that situation. So that anything you do is right.
Anything you do, that is to say, is unexpected and yet
it coheres. Anything you have the character say has
that ring of the unexpected, of discovery, because
after all, we don't know what we're going to say next.
In other words, I can't get ahead of him. And if I can't

get ahead of him and yet he keeps talking, I know I've got something. If I can get too far ahead of him and simply report what I already know through his mouth, the play is a dead duck. Now, I believe that this has very little to do with what we call psychology. I've said this to many people: I'm not a good psychologist. In other words, when I observe people I'm often taken in by them or often suspect those who give no reason at all to be suspected. My appraisal of them is the last thing that I would advise anybody to consult. What does it mean? It means simply that there are certain people into whom I can project myself. I can tell them before they say it what they're going to say. Most people I can't do that with; there are only a few. You only need a few because whether it's Shakespeare or anybody else, the number of human principles involved are finite, but the variations one can play upon them are infinite. I suppose you could give the process a good name called projection, but it has nothing to do with psychology in a sense of judging or weighing or discovering objective principles of how or why people behave. That's the end result, and now I'm talking about the process. The objective fact is the work itself. That is in a profound way no longer the author's property. That's the audience's. And what he has revealed in terms of objective laws or objective clues to some generalization about mankind is almost an aftereffect, in a good way. The works that set out to do this usually lack life. They are dead, so one of the reasons why I have such a small horizon for psychology is the dialectic involved. In order to draw a conclusion, you have to arrive yourself into an area where no conclusions are visible. You have to die in order to live, so to speak. You have to be blind in order to see. And that is why a writer has to be disassociated from his work in that respect. Plato was right. We don't know what we are doing. Everything I say about my plays is a rationalization after the fact. The best proof of it is that I started writing *Death of a Salesman* one day in Connecticut. I wrote the whole play. Then, in one of my annual fits of neatness, I decided to clean out closets, suitcases, and so on, and make what I call order. This usually lasts for four or five days and then collapses, and everything has simply been moved from one place to another. And in the course of that I discovered old notebooks, and in one old notebook which dated back to 1936 when I was at college, there was a play about a salesman of which I'd written an act and a half. All these characters were there in a different form, but they were the same people, and obviously I had been striving as a student to start to grapple with this material. I had completely forgotten that I had written an act and a half of the play. Thank God I had forgotten it because it wasn't good and it would have discouraged me if I had found it too early. I'm saying the obvious, which is that we're bound by a certain unconscious continuity. It's the main thing, which again brings us back to the business of uniqueness because fiction is such, drama certainly is, and what you want is raw material. You don't want what I think about something, not really, because what I think about something is far from unique. But the creation of life is what you're after, and that is something that you can't will. I think that's why people want the theater as much as they do, or why they want art of any kind. They want evidence of this sense of life.

EVANS: Now, to pursue this idea of the writer's conception of the audience for which the play is intended, let's discuss *Death of a Salesman* further. You've used an impressionistic form; that is, you deliberately put the play together with hopes for considerable latitude in the range of audience interpretation or conjecture. As you mentioned earlier, you didn't want to spell things out too precisely so you could hopefully elicit the emotional affect that we were just discussing. Then the film was made in Hollywood, and suddenly this impressionistic technique disappeared. The film people apparently thought more precise realism and more stereotyped characterization were necessary in order to reach a broader audience.

MILLER: That is a very interesting phenomenon, by the way.

EVANS: Yes. Now at this point the possibilities for empathy began to be downgraded somewhat, were they not?

MILLER: I'll tell you why. Exactly why. It impinges directly upon psychology, too, by the way, and upon the age we're living in. You see, I never conceived Willy as being crazy. Willy was a human being to me. He was not a set of symptoms. He was never crazy, not to the end of his life. There was even a certain rational rule in his decision to kill himself. What they did (and I will go into why they did it) was that when they made the film of *Salesman*, they showed a man who is nuts from the first reel. He starts as a pathological case, and he only had the interest of a pathological case because you couldn't identify yourself with a pathological case; that is almost a definition of a pathological case. They did not film *Salesman*, but their conclusions about it. Their Willy has sprung loose from anything we call normal human behavior. Now why did they do that? I have here a proof which is interesting. At that time the United States was entering the Cold War. It was just at the point—1950—where things began to get very tight. Now they went and made this picture in which they had invested several millions of dollars and with it, unknown to me, they made a twenty-minute short which was to be shown at all the theaters in conjunction with *Death of a Salesman*. And what was the short about? That short, which I'm sure cost them at least $150,000 to make, showed that in reality, salesmen were one of the most secure, honored groups in society. It was made by Columbia Pictures without my knowledge. However, they were by contract not permitted to do this without my permission. When they finished the picture, they asked me to okay showing it in the theaters, and of course I forbade the showing of this thing in conjunction with my play because it made the whole play seem like a complete fabrication or a piece of stupidity if nothing else. And they never showed it. Now the two things go together. They couldn't bear the thought that a normal man in the society might be driven to these extremes; he had to be crazy to start with. That was what I'd call a psychological approach to reality, when it's mishandled and distorted and disfigured in this way. Do you see what I mean? In other words, the movie is *Death of a Salesman* as it would be done by people who had no artistry and too much "psychology." But they knew how to get society off the hook.

EVANS: Perhaps their estimate of the target group, the broader audience that would see this film, was that they wouldn't be able to cope with this picture of themselves.

MILLER: That's right.

EVANS: So therefore, they've got to disassociate the characters from the audience.

MILLER: I'll go even further. The people who made the film couldn't cope with the thing themselves; they couldn't bear it. As a matter of fact, I only advised them from time to time during the writing of the screenplay. They'd send me forty or fifty pages and I'd send them back and say, "It's dreadful. You've got to start all over again." And their answers were always the same. I remember one specifically. There was a scene with Biff, the older son, talking to the mother in a hostile way. It's a passage of eight or ten lines which sets up the whole scene. You know what they said? They said, "We can't have him talking to his mother like that." In other words, here were what they called little changes being made which resulted in an abortion. The whole thing had no validity either as psychology or as art or as entertainment or as anything. Basically their ineptitude stemmed from fear that a sane Willy would, in effect, shake society.

EVANS: I think that most people looking realistically at Willy in the play see him as Everyman, in a sense. And the play comes to grips finally with the existential question: Who am I? Perhaps as an art form, the motion picture has changed enough today so that if they were to remake the film, they may feel that audiences would be ready for this. Certainly the recent television version in which you were personally more deeply involved was highly successful, even though it stuck tenaciously to the spirit of the play.

MILLER: I think that is true. But my previous experience shows that we're not talking about something in our own minds or something academic or something that does not have real cogency for people who have to administer certain power and have to accomplish certain things in this world. They can't face the truth; it's simply something they can't bear to do. So that is why art exists. To do what people can't do and what they must do if they're to proceed truthfully.

EVANS: I think this is a very interesting example; it is almost a case history of the various things we were talking about. What we're really saying is that apparently the impact was so great that here are people willing to try to protect the audience or in a sense society from that impact. It is almost testimony to the strength of the impact.

MILLER: They can't bear it themselves. They are the first ones that can't bear it. You see if they could bear it, it wouldn't occur to them that other people couldn't bear it. Do you see what I mean?

EVANS: Yes, of course. As I mentioned earlier when we were discussing the possibilities for the emotional growth of members of a play's audience, this whole problem of measuring audience reaction is a tough one. We don't know very much about it yet in the artistic media such as the theater. Every once in a while, for example, I talk to someone in a local theater group who says something like, "We'd like to learn something about our little theater and its potential success with audiences. We want to know more about our audiences in the sense of what various kinds of plays mean to them, what kind of plays they want." And I suspect that to some degree they are asking for information with which theatrical audiences may not be able to provide them in a form which would really be useful. That is, I'm not so sure that you can ask people, "What kind of plays do you really want to see?" and get a meaningful response.

MILLER: They wouldn't know.

EVANS: Or, "You just saw this play. What was its impact on you?" Again, the reaction may be something much more subtle than can be elicited by a question of this sort. I suspect you must have some way of gauging potential audience interest, comprehension and response, do you not?

MILLER: I suppose I do; I'd never put it that way to myself. I suppose somewhere in me is a sensitization, so to speak, in relation to the rest of mankind or to the rest of my coinhabitants of this area, anyway. There must be, or else I wouldn't know how to make anything clear to them. I must have some sense of what they understand and what they don't understand, what is too prolix, what is too naïve, and so on. But if I think of it at all, I think of it really in these terms, and that is, if I am moved by something and I can convey my emotion, they will be moved by it and that same emotion will be theirs.

EVANS: One of the very complex things about your

form of communication, which I think would be frightening in its complexity to people engaged in more direct forms of communication, like straight news broadcasting, for example, is that your play has to pass through so many interpretations. That is, the audience is on one side and you are on the other, and then in between you have to worry about the producer, the director, the set designer, the makeup man, the lighting man, and all the actors. In a sense, it's not just the audience you are talking to; you're talking to all of these middlemen. Psychologically, one would guess that a good deal of shaping and shifting and changing takes place. To what degree do you fear this process?

MILLER: It is a fear. All those elements are important, but none is as decisive as the actor. I don't think a director can hurt my plays, which are plays that don't depend upon effects, but depend more on the truth of characterizations. The director can't make you or break you, but an actor can come close to doing that. And it needn't be his fault or your fault. This is where we almost get into clinical psychology, because when I sit in an office with a director and a producer and interview actors, some of whom I've never seen before in my life, we just talk at random for twenty minutes, and I have to judge whether or not this man is capable of anger, whether he is capable of seeming he could love somebody as a tough and hardened individual or as a very sentimental and soft one. I have to make what I suppose a psychologist would call a clinical analysis of this man. Well, naturally the chances one takes in such a thing are immense; you may be absolutely wrong. The man comes in. He looks completely adequate. You put him up on the stage, and it's quite apparent he's a baby. But it only comes out when he has to pass through the emotional scenes that you put before him. Suddenly you see he has no equipment for them, or he has the wrong kind of equipment, so new tonalities come out. Now very often it's too late; you don't see these revealed in time. The nature of the beast is such that it takes the actor a while to develop the part so that his weaknesses are shown. You can't ask him to act in two days. It's impossible. By the time he's developed the part, it's too late. So you've got a performance that's a distortion to begin with. And if the play isn't strong enough, the performance can sink it. There's no question about it. Or it can make the play seem trivial when it isn't; it can give the play all kinds of tones that it never really had. And this is the playwright's nightmare.

EVANS: Of course, by the same token, you have another problem. Anyone can pick up one of your plays and merely read it without ever seeing it performed as you meant it to be. Would you be less worried about someone reading your play than seeing it badly done?

MILLER: I'd rather have them read it than have them see it badly done, yes. But as you know, a play is not written primarily to be read. It's to be played. There's not a real analogy; the closest thing I can think of perhaps is being able to read music, but that presupposes that a man is already a musician and can really hear in his mind what the music is, and most readers are not that accomplished.

EVANS: No. A conductor looking at a score might be able to do that, but the average listener can't.

MILLER: Yes. The playwright is stuck, and that's his situation. And that's the friction in the machine. The machine has to be strong enough to keep operating despite the fact that it's heating up like that.

EVANS: You seem to suggest that selecting the actor for a part is a pretty intuitive process. Do you think that somewhat more scientific objective techniques might be developed in order to help the producer, director, and playwright in selecting the "right" actor for the "right" role?

MILLER: I don't think it could be a science for one simple reason. Maybe I'm underestimating science, but you can't imagine the imponderables and the variety of influences upon an actor in relation to any particular role. There is too much to control. Aside from estimating him as a psychological or personality type there is something much more important, and impossible to gauge in advance—his talent.

THE WRITER AND PSYCHOLOGY

PART II

EVANS: To move now to a slightly different area, you have already pointed out that you don't really see characters as people. You get a series of impressions and pull them together in terms of a pattern that you have developed, and the realness of the person as he may appear to the audience is not an important thing to you. However, when one thinks about how a psychologist tries to describe a person, he sometimes falls short of describing a real person also. His tools are based on certain information he has gained which applies to most people, but certainly not *precisely* to every person. At this point, I'd like to get your reaction to a few ideas of various psychologists that might at least superficially be relevant to the task of the playwright as he develops his characters. We have one point of view, a non-Freudian one, developed by Gordon Allport, where he focused on personality traits as a means of understanding the individual. For example, he introduced the idea of cardinal traits; that is, the particular traits that most vividly characterize a particular person in addition to the common traits we share with all individuals. Let's say the cardinal traits that stand out in one individual are his compulsive honesty and integrity. This might be the way he is primarily characterized, a person with honesty and integrity. In another person, the things that stand out are his enthusiasm and vigor, and so on. Does such a trait approach make any sense to you?

MILLER: I'll tell you the way I look at it, and that is dialectically. In other words, what interests me about somebody may be a trait, but only a conflict bears writing about. Let's use the classic example of a miser. Miserliness is of no interest to me until I find out that under certain circumstances, the miser throws away money. He's absolutely uncontrollable in his waste of money or his effects, his wealth, his emotions. Then I start to get an outline of a living organism. Anything in itself is of no interest to me; it lacks usefulness. If somebody tells me that a person is cruel, I can't use it. I can use that point of conflict, that point of contradiction or paradox. You see, every play is built on a paradox. It must be; there is no other way to proceed that I know of without turning the play into a narrative which is the biggest trouble with many contemporary plays. A narrative need not have a paradox, but a drama must. For example, a character thinks he's doing exactly the opposite. If that paradox is not present, then there is no genuine movement, there is no engine in the play. The play needs dialectical relationships. It's the relationships between and within the people, and these relationships are dialectical; that is, one thing sets off another thing, which in turn sets off a third thing, and ad infinitum to a point of catharsis, where there is a synthesis of these contradictions, and the work challenges chaos with form.

EVANS: Interestingly enough, this is consistent with other psychological theories such as those of Harry Stack Sullivan, which also stress interpersonal relationships as the important focus. Another point of view in psychology to which it might be interesting to get your reaction is called field theory. Kurt Lewin argued that behavior is a function of what he called the life space. This consists of the totality of forces which impinge upon the person at any given moment, and from moment to moment all these forces change. Behavior is thus a function of forces impinging on the individual at any given moment. Lewin stated that the psychoanalytic focus on the past in order to understand the present (e.g., the first five years of life), although very interesting in perspective, was far less important than defining all the forces impinging on the individual at a given moment. Field theory also emphasizes the importance of mobility within our state of consciousness in that the individual may change levels of reality. He may shift from the present real world to images of the past and back again to the present, project the future, and so on. But the important focus in field theory is that all of these influences impinge on the person in the present. In another of your plays, *After the Fall*, you appear to be almost literally working at characterization from a field theoretical point of view.

MILLER: In a sense that is true of *Death of a Salesman* as well. Unless you are insane, I don't think you can really move out of the present; I think that to me that is one definition of insanity, that condition in which the hold on the immediate is gone. Then you say somebody is crazy; he doesn't know where he is, he's disoriented. But those two plays and also my other plays are built upon my sense of drama, which is that there is a terrific emotional tension within the person who is drawn back to the past in order to orient himself to the present. In a sense a good play is always the story of how the birds come home to roost. But when you leave the present altogether—as with mechanical flashbacks—you leave the drama for narrative.

EVANS: Let's consider a few other notions in personality psychology which may have relevance to your construction of a play. One of Carl Jung's interesting but controversial contributions is his idea of archetypes. He felt that from the primeval beginnings of man through a phylogenetic process certain universal behavior patterns of man were transmitted through a collective or race unconscious. Although the setting for the emergence of an archetype at any given point in the history of man may be different, these archetypes, which are universal and virtually infinite, are crucial to the patterns of man's existence. For example, the Mother, Evil, the Father, or the Hero are examples of such archetypes, which are reflected over and over in man from generation to generation.

MILLER: I think there's a great deal to that theory. I believe it as a writer because I can read stuff written four or five hundred years ago in completely different cultures, cultures with which I have very little or nothing in common, Chinese literature or something of that sort, and see that there are certain limited archetypes that recur. I don't think that there's any question about the validity of Jung's theory, but I wouldn't know, of course, what value it would be in therapy. He was working as a therapist, I assume.

EVANS: Partly that, but also partly as a theorist to try to understand the most fundamental basis of man's behavior.

MILLER: I think it's true, but I don't know where it would lead. There's a certain kind of mysticism involved in it which both attracts and repels me. I would imagine that as a theory it mostly explains itself, but there is a beauty in it, like reincarnation. Perhaps the attraction is that repetition implies form and form implies meaning. What repels me is an aspect of predestination in it that makes the will absurd, and struggle too. Also, it smells of hierarchy and the philosophicalness that leaves evil undisturbed. It seems like a viewpoint for the very successful or the totally defeated. Yet, there are types and there is no way around that.

EVANS: How do you regard Alfred Adler's notion that the individual is born with basic feelings of inferiority, and most individual behavior is in a sense directed toward overcoming these feelings of inferiority?

MILLER: That theory seems circular to me. I've never known a person who felt he was in some respect inferior, without a more or less good reason for feeling

that way. In a sense, everything we do is a compensa-
tion, a flight-from quite as much as a thrust-toward.
In other words, I fail to understand the paradox between feelings of inferiority and good health. Everything depends on what you make of it, so in itself it
doesn't seem an operative distinction. Besides, feelings
of inferiority seem more like an effect rather than a
cause. But in any case I don't have a theory although
I suppose I work from some construct that is repetitive, that is usable in play after play. I think that in
the plays, the people have some preconception of having been displaced from what they should be or even
of what they "really" are, and the tension consists in
their trying to arrive by one means or another at where
they "ought" to be. Before my plays start, there is a
preconception about the condition of the characters
and the sense that they're not in that condition and
are striving, sometimes unto death, to get into that
condition. I don't know what you would call that in
terms of what you've been speaking of, a general
theory, but it's as close as I can come to one. It's the
only prescription that I can think of at the moment,
and yet, it is not even useful to me to know that. It is
a recollection after the fact. I wouldn't know where
to use that in writing a new work.

EVANS: This is an interesting point because most
psychological researchers would ordinarily start with
a theory as they begin an exploration. You're implying
that starting with a theory could almost inhibit the
creative process of a playwright. Isn't this what you
are suggesting?

MILLER: Yes, that's the difference. What is involved here is that I feel I have certain evidence, like a witness before the world. And it would be tampering with the evidence to formulate it too soon; it would be making a case for it. My notebooks are filled with the evidence, and then I look at it and try to find the consistencies and the themes in it—a form.

EVANS: Could you give me some examples of some of this evidence, something you may be working on?

MILLER: In this notebook, which was done over the past month, are the beginnings of four different plays. They're all unrelated in terms of the people involved, but then suddenly the people in one play might start moving over to the story of another and then suddenly they change their identity altogether. One play might take place in a rooming house, another at a ball in Europe, and another in an army camp, and yet I know that because one man is writing all these unrelated bits and pieces, there must be some secretly consistent preoccupation underneath them all. And I slowly begin to move through these materials to find one single body for them.

EVANS: At this point I want to emphasize that I was using only a few of the ideas of Allport, Lewin, Jung, and Adler simply to get your reactions as a means of learning more about the way you approach the task of developing characterization and conflict in your plays. We could discuss many other ideas of these men, but critics have particularly applied psychoanalytic theory to your work so we might discuss Freud's notions in more detail.

MILLER: I am far from disparaging Freud, but in general I've found that there is a tendency to mechani-

cally apply everything that Freud discovered. But it is
equally true of Marx, St. Augustine, or any of the
other synthesizing people.

EVANS: Notwithstanding this general statement you
are making about the misapplications of Freud's ideas,
certainly many writers would see in your work a good
deal of psychoanalytical material. For example, psy-
choanalysts are interested in the unconscious and
guilt. They argue that the unfolding and development
of life is the progressive ability to handle guilt, among
other conflicts and frustrations. Psychoanalysis also
deals with ego defense mechanisms such as rationalization and projection. Psychoanalytically oriented
critics look at your work and feel that all of these
things seem to show themselves very dramatically in
your work. In *Death of a Salesman*, for instance, Willy
is a character in whom the unconscious appears to be
operating in a variety of his experiences and behavior
such as the fantasy of the uncle. There is the theme
of guilt stemming from his affair with the prostitute
and his son's discovery of this. Then there is rationalization: Willy always presents a good excuse rather
than the real reason for his failures. Do you think this
kind of interpretation, where a character like Willy is
regarded in even superficial psychoanalytical terms,
has any value?

MILLER: It depends upon how it is done. I haven't
read very much of what has been written about that
play or any of my plays, much as I realize that a lot
has been written, but what I've read about *Death of a
Salesman* was mixed. There is a misconception about
how a writer uses symbols, for example. I was as-

tounded to learn that Biff, the older son, steals a
fountain pen and that I had intended this to be a
phallic symbol. Well, fountain pens can be phallic
symbols, but really, what does it say about anything?
I had no thought of such a thing. In fact, I would say
that an author who is trying to fill preconceived symbols is defeating himself, because what we really want
from a work of art is evidence, new evidence, new
raw material. We don't want a finger exercise of some
sort which fills out a preconceived pattern; it's false,
learned behavior. A critic might write that way, but a
writer ought not to do it. So that my personal attitude
is curiosity about what psychologists make of the
material, but a suspension of disbelief, so to speak; I
wonder sometimes what help it is to anybody to have
all those pieces of structural information, structural in
the sense that they conform to a Freudian psychology
or don't conform to it. It seems to me that a lot of
people have gotten lost in making this analysis an end
in itself. After all, a play is written for moral reasons,
too, and sometimes plays are written, some very good
works, as much because the writer wants to reorganize
the world morally or to discover what he believes is
a hidden set of forces which are death forces in the
world and others which are life forces; that's all morality is, after all, the discovery of a way to live in cele-
bration of life rather than giving way to death; that
first preoccupation was a minor one. I think Goethe
was very often that kind of a writer. He wanted to
make a moral order out of what is chaos. He was trying to invite the attention of the universe to the insignificant man by claiming some kind of recognition

from the universe. This is rather hard to enclose in a purely psychological or even a basically psychological approach. My point is that I would want psychology to refer itself more and more to literature, more and more to life, rather than to refer itself back to psychology. I think there is a danger that psychology is becoming the literature, that the so-called scientific view of man and motivation is becoming the literature of the twentieth century. My point is that there is a growing tendency not only to substitute psychoanalysis or psychological analysis for art, but to regard it as the prime source of information about man, and I don't believe in it. I don't believe in it because it perceives too much from the conscious mind. I think we know as much information that we are not aware we know as the opposite. And I would like to see science in general become cultured again, because it is in the area of felt knowledge that progress lies, it seems to me. I think psychologists and artists both can perceive in their own fields, but there is a tendency for one to take over the other, and even the artists in many cases feel that they are in a dying profession. That is, that they should become critics or that they are really critics once removed, intead of the other way around; it's an evil because it disfigures both fields.

EVANS: C. P. Snow, in his discussion of two cultures, the scientific and the humanistic, presents similar problems and suggests that there are difficulties in communication between the two. But there is a question here that isn't quite resolved by your statement. Let's say that you arrive at a brilliant understanding of the unconscious in some of your work, and that this understanding also appeared in Freud's work. Now, regardless of whether it is labeled Freudian or not, this understanding is being used to develop a characterization and perhaps to teach and to contribute to the emotional growth we were discussing earlier in the person who sees your play. Now whether or not we call it Freudian, a concept of the unconscious or of guilt might very well be important as you look at Willy. You are being psychological whether you are doing it in a superficial extrapolative sense or in a more broadly profound creative sense. Now this, as a matter of fact, is one reason that I think many have reacted to some of your plays so intensely. Without regard to what label we want to put on it, you are arriving at a kind of truth and that truth happens to be similar in many ways to the kind of truth that Freud and many other psychoanalytic writers have discovered. Would you agree with this interpretation?

MILLER: Yes, if it is that much a part of my equipment, so to speak. In my opinion, Freud's achievement is something you would have to call the result of cultural or moral commitment of a sort. It may not be easy to spell it out. It is not the scientific idea of the objective, detached observer who needs part of the engine that describes Freud's whole effort; it was the fact that he lived in a certain culture, that he was a Jew, that he was what he was and that society was what it was. In other words, this was not the discovery of penicillin. Do you see what I mean? I could even make similar statements about the discovery of penicillin, by the way, but it certainly was true in Freud's

case. He was a species of artist because he was working intuitively much of the time; that's one of the
reasons he is criticized, I think. But it is only through
exploring the unknown in oneself that one comes up
with anything new, it seems to me, and there is a
great tendency in these times for the psychologist to
rejuggle concepts anew without endangering himself
personally, laying himself on the line in this respect.
There is too much thinking in terms of controlling
man rather than freeing him, of defining him rather
than sensing him. And it's part of the whole ideology
of this power-mad age. I think we are all nuts in one
respect, and that is that everybody conceives of success or his own accomplishment in terms of some sort
of power. And there is no reason psychology shouldn't
be affected by that too, except that you are scientists
and should be aware of it. But to get back to your
question, the fact that any of my works bear out
Freud or not doesn't seem to me to make it more
artistic or less. My reference point is not of that kind.

EVANS: But to introduce another perspective here
for a moment, I think we might say that the question
of the creative process may be involved in much of
what we have been discussing. What I'm asking you
is whether or not you think the playwright's formal or
informal knowledge of psychological theory is related
to his creation of a drama. You've said that maybe it
doesn't contribute very much. Would you say, therefore, that a dramatist should not read psychology and
not become acquainted with these theories, that perhaps it is most important not to inhibit intuition?
Would you say that it might even cripple his thinking
to become aware of these formal theories?

MILLER: I wouldn't go that far because there are some writers, like Eugene O'Neill, who obviously read Freud at a certain point and used him quite openly, although in my opinion, too mechanically, in certain of his works. My personal capacity to absorb formal psychological information—theoretical information— is very low. If I read a theory of personality, if I read Freud—which I've never been able to do at any length —my mind immediately starts seeking examples in my own experience of what he is talking about. And very shortly I come up with a whole shimmering dialectic of my own which makes me say, "Well, his decision about what is making this tick is good, but it could be a lot of other things." In other words, I'm not in the business of therapy. I'm in the business of creating life, which is again raw material. So that whether or not a writer should read this stuff, I can't read it. It just doesn't register. I've had many opportunities to do it. People send me theses and books they have written, sometimes having to do with my work, and I find that I can follow the logic but it's basically unusable. I can't use it. It's like a screen from outside placed over me, and I'm struggling to get out of it. I can't operate that way; it's of no use to me at all. Now I will add, though, that I was brought up and I lived in a time when psychiatric and Freudian theory were in the air. You got into a taxicab, and the driver begins to tell you a story and makes psychiatric comments on it. He's not aware that he's making them, but he is. Everybody knows this stuff now, so that this is part of my reality. It's part of my background as much as anything I've read, if not more so, so it's not quite fair to say that I exist to one side of psychological knowledge, or that I've been independent of it. That wouldn't be true. However, I would be inclined to say that a formal education in psychology wouldn't be of any help to a man who writes because that isn't where your stuff comes from; I'm not a writer because I learn certain things. I'm a writer because I am certain things, and I think it's too instinctive a process to be reached by that kind of information, you see; or at least, so it is with me. Now another writer who is working from a different part of his psyche possibly could be helped by it.

EVANS: The fact that you feel that creative people may work in different ways and presumably all you can do is to speak from your own personal experience is certainly a fair qualification here.

MILLER: Of course, knowledge can't hurt, except at particular moments. Sometimes it's better not to know certain things. I suppose if I'd known too much, there are certain things I wouldn't have written which I'm glad I wrote. I'd leave it at that. Just an ability to speak through the stage is a very delicate business. You can't kick it around too much. You've got to come back to what you know, to what you've written, to what you really feel because that's what the audience wants. They want the unique evidence of one spirit in this time, and they don't want their own opinions rearranged and regurgitated by somebody who is expert at them. It's the nature of the art, I think. It's why you go to the theater. I suppose you are all aware of this. I don't follow psychology, and I know very little about it, but if you want to turn to art as a source of wisdom in your field, I think that the main thing to face is the idea that the writer, the artist, is interested in a total rendition of all the dynamics that are involved in the man in the situation. His art consists in suggesting those things. My argument with so much that passes for psychology and even psychoanalysis is that instead of seeking a systhesis in man, it seems to be driving toward a partitioning of man, which I think is probably unscientific finally because it's like studying the moment of explosion of some chemical without studying the chemical in a state of rest and in other states of heat and cold. You can't get anywhere that way. It seems to me to falsify the nature of man. What I am asking for is a certain humility before the problem which would then make it impossible for people simply to use a certain kind of terminology in relation to human actions and human psychology and feel that since they know the name for something, they understand it.

EVANS: You are touching on a very vital point that concerns us even in training students. In the history of the treatment of mental illnesses, psychopathologists came up with a systematic classification of mental disorders and their symptoms. The reason for these labels was simply to make the diagnostician and therapist more efficient. That is, if several different people have a given kind of disorder, let's say schizophrenia, and a particularly successful way of treating that disorder is developed, that opens a door. It's really an application of the medical model of diagnosis and treatment. What you are saying is that these labels are misused and sometimes description is substituted for understanding. I think many of us would share your views that too many individuals in this field fall into the trap of confusing the description or labeling of an illness, with really understanding it. In fact, labels may actually interfere with cures.

MILLER: The worst thing about these labels is that they pass into the currency of the culture. Without these words, people might be driven by their bewilderment to try to come to some understanding; just the tension of not understanding might make them go further. But they come upon these concepts which are ready-made and seem to fit, and then they use them as weapons against each other. It is a kind of word duel that takes the place of any real human relationship between them. I've seen that happen many times with people who've been analyzed. They come out of the analysis covered with labels and tags, and they cut each other up with the tags.

EVANS: I agree. One of the unfortunate by-products of these classifications in psychiatry is that they have provided the layman with a new variety of name-calling. In fact, the field itself is actually going beyond this. Less and less faith in the value of classifying and labeling mental disorders characterizes most of the creative professionals in this field.

MILLER: I'm speaking out of a kind of ignorance which is inexcusable, but which at the same time is what you are up against, but I think that there's a false objectivity that is surrounding some of this stuff, if you don't mind my saying it, I think that everybody has a point of view. I think it's impossible not to have a point of view about human psychology. You may not have one about physics or chemistry, but there can't really be a direct or physical relationship between what happens in that complicated brain of ours and what happens in a test tube. It's impossible. And consequently, one does have a view of man, what he should be, what he is. And if psychologists aired what they think a man really ought to be—embarrass themselves a little bit, you see—psychology would cease to be quite as much of a blanket for the psychologist. You have to suffer to discover anything. Let me put it that way. I sometimes sense a want of suffering. There is another thing I can't detach from the study of man, too. I'll give you an example of what I am talking about. The ultimate questions involved in any study of man, either psychological or esthetic, are questions of value, of course. I'll tell you a story which happened five or six years ago. I was prevailed upon to appear just to make some comments at a meeting of the American Psychological Association. I didn't make a speech, but two people did and Jim Farrell and I were there just to say what we thought about the subject of creativity. Both of us said a lot of nonsense, but at one point I made a remark about a Nazi doctor in the concentration camp who decided that it would be interesting to hold somebody under water for a certain amount of time and see what the physiological reactions were as he was drowning, because obviously we have never studied anybody drowning. We've studied him after he's drowned, but they carried on such experiments. That was the least of them; there were many others that were worse. Afterwards, when I was leaving the room, fifteen to twenty people, most of them women by the way, stopped me, and one woman said, "Well, why isn't that science?" Now this wasn't in Munich or Berlin; this was in New York. And I think that is a very important question; it goes to the heart of a lot of studying that's going on. I'm not here to tell you why I think it is science, but I think if it is science, then we'd better rethink the whole basis of what we're doing, and whether it is simply to create a world that is valueless, because there is no such thing as a non-point-of-view. The man that says "I have no point of view" is expressing a point of view. And it seems to me that at the heart of good research there has to be some commitment to man. It is a failing of the intellect and of the heart to obliterate that. And finally, it won't even be good science; I think it probably will end up as bad science.

EVANS: The questions of the role of values in science and of detachment in the scientist have plagued every scientist. In fact, many contemporary psychologists such as Abraham Maslow, Carl Rogers, and Erich Fromm would share your concern. They would certainly state that psychologists should begin with a humanistic commitment—that the psychologist cannot hide behind a veil of pseudo-objectivity.

MILLER: I don't want that question to get lost, because whatever we say here is really impinging on it.

EVANS: We can certainly return to it later, but at this point let's turn to another facet of the subject. Psychologists have developed various formal concepts of personality and we have your reactions to a few of these formal psychological notions, and how they do or do not apply to what you are doing, but there's another interesting side of a play besides characterization per se. That is its so-called message. In a sense we might say that *The Crucible* or *All My Sons* has a message. We're presumably talking about your attempt somehow to have an effect on the attitudes and ideologies of the individuals seeing your play. Since social psychologists have engaged in research concerning the nature and impact of messages, it might be interesting to compare our views of messages and their impact. First of all, do you believe that you have "messages" in some of your plays?

MILLER: I don't like that word because I don't think a message, in the sense that you're sending a telegram, has any use or effect whatsoever. In *The Crucible*, to give a specific example, I was using a certain form and a certain historical period. When I was in college, I studied American history, and I was struck by the incident in Salem that happened years before I wrote anything about it.

EVANS: So you first began thinking of this back in the thirties?

MILLER: Yes, in thirty-five and thirty-six. And I never thought of making a play out of it. It just was a fascinating thing to me that a town of this kind could suddenly erupt in explosive hysteria. I just couldn't understand how it could happen. It was like reading about some creatures on the moon, and I forgot about it. Well, the whole attitude of the fifties started to develop. People were persecuted, and they were jumping out of windows. Friendships were being destroyed. There were disasters all around. The repetitiousness of it brought up the idea of the Salem witchcraft trials, where on a different level with different folkways essentially the same phenomenon was occurring. I was led back by a memory that was perhaps fifteen or twenty years old, and in which I'd already invested some emotion. It was no longer like something learned, you see; I had almost invented the witchcraft by this time. I wanted to tell people what had happened before and where to find the early underlying forces of such a phenomenon. In this respect, perhaps we can discuss Jung's idea of archetypes further.

EVANS: So you believe this phenomenon to be an archetype then?

MILLER: Yes, I would say it is. When A happens and B happens and then C happens and D happens, it is almost inevitable that E is going to happen. Now we're standing over the abyss, and you are about to witness the final act of the old disaster, and that's how that play began to develop. But into that structural idea goes a lot of personal feeling about men and women and about marriage. One playwright saw it, and he said, "This play's about marriage." Well, it is a curious thing, isn't it, that the message then is still very important. The National Theatre, Olivier's theater in England, played *The Crucible* for a year, and it is also in the repertory theater that they have in London. Olivier told me that it's a great hit there, and a good half of the audience has little awareness that the play had any root in a contemporary American situation. In fact, many people in the audience were overheard saying, "They say that this has got something to do with McCarthy." Now you see what you call a message can be very important in the structuring of a work, but its meaning can change if it is a living thing. It's not only important to my work, but it goes down through history. We see *The Magic Flute*. It would take a real scholar to find the defense of Freemasonry in Mozart's operas, and yet at the time, this was a central preoccupation of Mozart and his librettist. The structure of the work was in great part determined by their preoccupation with proving something about Freemasory. It's important but ultimately, it's beside the point compared to the life it gives birth to in the work at hand.

EVANS: Perhaps we could make a distinction between the statement of a pervasive, eternal truth about man and the writer's immediate need to persuade or propagandize his audience over some issue of current importance to him. Perhaps you are saying that if the writer is merely satisfying the immediate need to persuade with respect to a current issue of importance to him, he doesn't really have an art form at all; he's got to be stating something much more pervasive and enduring even though it appears to be focused on a current issue threatening to him.

MILLER: The writer must be in it; he can't be to one side of it, ever. He has to be endangered by it. His own attitudes have to be tested in it. The best work that anybody ever writes is the work that is on the verge of embarrassing him, always. It's inevitable. Where he puts himself on the line, sometimes quite secretly, sometimes symbolically. But without that implication of the writer himself, a truth has not been served. He's formulated something that's quite safe and about which he doesn't care quite enough. Prophecy written from abroad, so to speak.

EVANS: One of your most recent plays, *Incident at Vichy*, also presents a message. Would what you have said about *The Crucible* also apply to this play?

MILLER: Yes, and it would apply to *Salesman*, too. I went through the notes that I made while I was writing that play, and I was quite surprised some years later to find that most of the notes had to do with what I would have wanted Willy to do that he wasn't doing. I was laying up a standard of some kind against him. I was trying to find out what man should be under these circumstances, how he could possibly act differently, in order to survive with some kind of human value. In other words, there's a constant testing of that structure to see whether it's sound or not, to measure it against opposing structures. And *Incident at Vichy* was taken to mean that I was against Nazism. And of course it's only because I'm dealing with a theme that I dealt with in *After the Fall*, which was quite simply that when we live in a time of great murders, we are inhabiting a world of murder for which we share the guilt. There are actions that we call nonactions, and we have what I won't call a moral responsibility for but rather a literal blood connection with the evil of the time; we have an investment in evils that we manage to escape, that sometimes those evils that we oppose are done in our interest. And what happens is simply that by virtue of these circumstances, a man is faced with his own complicity with what he despises.

EVANS: Speaking of this play, *Incident at Vichy*, I can't resist one question that's somewhat more specific than most of the others. What are you attempting to portray by your presentation of the psychoanalyst, who passes a severely negative judgment on the Prince for his connections with the Nazis, and the sequence of events which follows including a kind of role reversal involving the psychoanalyst and the Prince?

MILLER: Not merely a reversal of roles. The Prince, during his time on stage, in the situation of a suspected Jew, realizes in his flesh, so to speak, what anti-Semitism meant. But he himself had always opposed the Nazis. Yet, as a Gentile they had spared him personally, and in his having survived by accident, so to speak, he now experiences an upsurge of guilt. Particularly because, as it turns out, he still feels the bond of human affection and even love for one of his cousins who, among other things, was an anti-Semitic Nazi. Until now his cousin's anti-Semitism did not seem to be the man's essence. To this degree, the Prince "understands" the destructive force and knows that it is in him. This love, this partaking of evil, is finally his responsibility; it is not something taking place outside him, and he cannot let it remain undisturbed within him. He wishes to extirpate it because it implies a complicity with everything he despises, and he substitutes himself for the psychoanalyst, he gives the doctor his own pass to freedom. But with that pass goes his guilt, and the doctor in accepting it, in accepting his own survival, is himself caught in complicity with the destruction of another man—the Prince, and guilt goes on. And indeed it does go on while there is injustice. So it is not a question merely of psychological insight, do you see? It is not enough to understand oneself, and this is the tragedy of social injustice, this is finally what it does to people, and even the psychoanalyst who understands himself cannot surmount it. The play was thought to be an arraignment of Nazism, but it is obviously far more than that. And incidentally, it taught me all over again what barriers people have to understanding their own relationship to injustice. As well as how little is understood about the ongoing implications of Nazism.

EVANS: This might be an appropriate point at which to discuss some specific conflict resolutions in your plays. Without referring necessarily to any particular theory of personality, there are psychological factors in characterization that seem to run through many of your plays. For example, you just mentioned the theme of guilt and how a character in *Incident at Vichy* handles it; however, how a character resolves guilt certainly seems to show itself more conspicuously in *All My Sons* and *Death of a Salesman*. In those two particular plays, the guilt is resolved by suicide. As a matter of fact, the suicide itself almost reflects some growth in each character. Of course, this seems to be kind of antithetical, that suicide can represent the growth of a character. We are led to believe as we see your characters that somehow the world, as well as they, themselves, is better for their having committed suicide.

MILLER: Put it this way: there is some growth that is intolerable, as there is some wisdom that is insufferable. It's insupportable for its very truth. This is exactly the case in *Incident at Vichy*. You see, I don't believe in the necessarily upgoing, ongoing, therapeutic power of wisdom. I think sometimes, at a certain point, one learns something that is true, profound, and intolerable, and which the person cannot support. There is an illumination that kills. That's where we get into an area called tragedy, which I don't suppose psychology can deal with because it seems to defeat everything. The problem is for me, of course, that it exists.

EVANS: After *Death of a Salesman*, however, there seems to be a different kind of conflict resolution in your characters; that is, you no longer resolve situations with the suicide of the principal character. Although one of the characters in *After the Fall* commits suicide, a remaining character shows a resolution of his personality conflict that would be much closer to the prevailing conception of mental health. Now, is there any particular reason why you portray this apparent shift in conflict resolution?

MILLER: Well, yes. You see, I think that all suicide victims are murdered. They are the victims of aggression, or sometimes the victims of truth that is in the form of a weapon. You see, Willy is really killed by the facts delivered to him by his sons and by the conditions of the development of their lives. So is the father in *All My Sons*. But somebody delivers the knowledge to these people, describes the situation to them so that it's remorseless and inescapable. In *After the Fall*, that kind of truth is delivered by Quentin in the sense that he cannot go on living with the illusion that Maggie has. Without that illusion, Maggie dies, She can't support her life. And yet, the tragic fact is that it means she dies alone, or they both go down, or whoever can, saves himself. It's obvious in these plays that there is the ironical question of the power of the truth to kill, to murder. And maybe this has formed some of my attitudes toward psychology which, perhaps mistakenly, are that there lies behind so much of it a preconception that, provided we know enough about ourselves, everything is going to turn out all right, that suffering is a mistake or a sign of weakness or the unfit, or a sign even of illness, when in fact, possibly the greatest truths we know have come out of suffering. The problem is not to undo suffering or to wipe it off the face of the earth, but to make it inform our lives so that we regard it as a necessary part of existence and try to pluck from it what growth and wisdom we can, instead of trying to cure ourselves of it constantly and to avoid it, and to avoid tension, avoid conflict, and arrive at that lobotomized sense of what they call happiness in which nobody learns anything but an ultimate, informed indifference. My plays are antipsychological in that respect, *Incident at Vichy* being perhaps the most open example. You see, I'm using the word psychological in its worst sense; in the sense, for example, of people who feel that King Lear was perhaps a study in senility. He's this mistake. You see, I don't think these people are faced with the exigencies of real existence, of really caring about where they are, of caring about others, of being intimately reached by the chaos in the universe. Perhaps I'm really drawing on a vulgarization, but it is a powerful and pervasive vulgarization.

EVANS: Yes, I believe you are right. By the time a lot of such thinking is interpreted into the popular culture, it's badly distorted. This is not what I think

Freud and most of the other significant contributors to psychological thought are talking about.

MILLER: Freud's mind was tragically oriented. In everything I've read about him or by him, there's always at the end of the vision that vacant spot where he knows he's defeated, but he wants then to be defeated with dignity. Do you see? He can't cure everybody. He may not even have an answer, but, by God, he's going to try with great dignity and all the intelligence and feeling he's got to arrive at some wisdom. But there's a reserve, a humility behind it. There's a sense that it's going to take the millennia before anybody learns anything and that it is still necessary never to stop trying.

EVANS: One thing I must say, though, in terms of Freud's developmental model—his idea of step-by-step development—he suggests that the way the individual learns about reality is through frustration; if we want to, we may call this suffering. Growth only comes through frustration and conflict, and, of course, conflict resolution. But he believed that we can only *approach* a conflict-free existence, not truly attain it. In a sense then, he's saying exactly what you're saying. What you're reacting to may not be what the sophisticated students of human development, such as Freud, are *really* saying, but with what people who have been analyzed unsuccessfully come away. The notion that there's such a thing as a tension-free state, that there's such a thing as absolute happiness, is something *no* sophisticated psychotherapist would suggest. You're right. I think that a lot of this type of distortion of psychological knowledge has come into our culture, but in a way I think you're very profoundly agreeing with the best insights of sophisticated psychotherapists.

MILLER: I am really arguing a related case—I don't think it serves any good purpose for the arts to be regarded as a handmaiden of psychiatry or psychology; obviously, the stuff you're dealing with is the stuff that the artist has from time immemorial been developing in terms of forms, and it's his bread and butter. God knows there are as many bad artists as there are bad psychologists, but there are a couple of good ones that are to me the authority, and I hate to see the frequent implication that they and their tragic outlooks are a kind of defective therapy.

EVANS: To move to another area, again as a means to focus on some of your work, there is today a great deal of concern and interest in what is called role conflict. In *Death of a Salesman*, we might argue that Willy is a father, and there's something special in this relationship with his sons that perhaps plays the most crucial part in his character development. Then we have Willy as a husband, and we have Willy as a salesman to complete the picture. These roles come into conflict at certain points, and you write very brilliantly about these conflicts. Now, in the study of personality we look for an integration of these roles. Although the roles are all here, they present a facade. Somehow, there has to be an underlying integration; otherwise we have nothing. Now is this need to integrate the various roles of a person an important force in trying to create a character in a play?

MILLER: In most of my plays, yes. Sometimes, as in *Incident at Vichy*, that kind of integration is left implied, but the attempt is always there.

EVANS: This mode of thought is really quite consistent with the essence of a lot of personality theory. In a way psychologists try to understand the integration of personality and are coping with perhaps the same thing that you are when you are trying to develop a character with impact.

MILLER: The direction is the same, probably, but the great and telling difference is the question of intention. I'm attempting to create life, and you're creating an analytical attitude toward it which is useful in curing disease or in some other way. I have no ulterior reason for what I am doing, you see. It's done because I need to make something beautiful, namely whole, and the rest is interesting but it's of secondary importance.

THE WRITER AND SOCIETY

PART III

EVANS: We might continue our discussion with a problem that I think is a very difficult one for the average psychology student. It centers around this problem: can we develop a true science of psychology? We have one point of view, behaviorism, which contends that there is no truly scientific way to deal with what's "under the skin" in the human organism—what the individual experiences. This should lead us to focus on predicting and controlling man's responses, since the responses man makes are observable physical units just like the matter which is examined in physics and chemistry. By manipulating the environmental contingencies which evoke these responses, we can learn to predict and control man's behavior. As we mentioned earlier, another view proposes a more humanistic emphasis which, although recognizing the difficulties of engaging in the scientific study of man while maintaining a humanistic stance, would argue that a humanistic position which includes the study of man's subjective experience is an indispensable part of understanding the individual. It brings up the question of whether or not the behaviorists should attempt to control or predict human behavior without fully understanding it. In your earlier remarks concerning your experience at the American Psychological Association meeting, you were already reacting negatively to the mechanistic view of the behaviorists and expressed fears concerning a psychology which teaches us to scientifically search for means of controlling man but fails to reflect a humanistic compassion for man. Would you care now to expand on your views of this problem?

MILLER: I admit that it raises a certain alarm in me, and a lot of doubt. For example, in my opinion, the problem of living today is not so much one of control as it is one of decontrol. It would seem to me that if you want to control people, I should imagine that history shows various ways of doing it pretty well. You can do it by terrifying them, or you can do it by punishing them. The Nazis did that, and they did it fairly well. If you did anything that was outside the rules, you got your head knocked off. The Communists have done it in various places from time to time. It can be done. The question is the value of the person that come out of these various attempts: How human he ends up being, how human he thinks he is, how human you think he is. From my point of view, there's no point asking what the efficaciousness of a technique is but what it is you're after. I have no opinions about those techniques. I don't know the easiest way to control people, or to make them do what you think they ought to do, or what we might think they ought to do. I do have views about what human behavior consists in, in the best sense of the word, and what inhuman behavior or ahuman behavior consists in. I must say in advance, the possibilities of really shaping people by scientific means, I think, are ultimately doomed. And I say that only because every child is born primitive; he is a threat to injustice because biologically he wants his share. You've got to start from scratch with every generation, and there are too many unforeseen possibilities. I think that the possibilities are infinite and that they're going to get away from you, finally. I have trouble myself if I try to figure out why I do what I do; it would be pretty hard, and I know a lot more about myself than a lot of people know about themselves.

EVANS: Let me play the devil's advocate for a moment. Some psychologists would argue this way: they'd say, "Well, we try to predict and/or control behavior employing maximum scientific objectivity, rigor, and exactness, so that our conclusions are valid. If you allow a humanistic dimension in the value system of the researcher to influence the study of man, you are building up 'noise' in the hopefully objective, experimental system that can't be controlled. Thus, one can't conduct research which yields reliable data." In other words, for all practical purposes then, you're eliminating psychology as a scientific discipline. Are you saying that we should do that?

MILLER: I sense that an attempt is being made despite everything to find *the* system or a system from which human behavior cannot escape, so to speak. It

sends chills up my back, to tell you the truth. I would
much rather that people spent their time asking: what
does it consist of to be human? How can science advance man toward that goal? Of course, I don't think
that this approach obliterates the scientific approach.
I think it makes science more difficult, but I wouldn't
say that it obliterated it. The "noise" in these systems
may simply be humanity trying to get out of them.

EVANS: Well, let me be a little bit more specific.
In your characterizations, you've shown us what you
think makes a human being human, and your views
are based not on scientific discourse but on a complex
intuitive perceptiveness and ability to understand and
integrate what you observe. If you were going to tell
a psychology student what you think makes a person
human, what would you say?

MILLER: I don't quite know how I would state that
in a syllogistic way; maybe it can be done. I don't
think you can differentiate human behavior, though,
in pure terms of drives. Sex, hunger, fear, and so on
are shared by other species. Even the capacity to build
is not ours alone, and some animals are even monoga-
mous, evidently. I think you have to reach out beyond such drives to social and even ethical impulses
to find the differences. Some will define man as the
animal most likely to destroy his own kind, and on
the record this is hard to knock down. But there is
also a countervailing impulse, an impulse toward
changing his environment in order to enhance life,
and doing so in a conscious way. This also differenti-
ates us. Perhaps a possible definition is that what
makes a person human is the conflict in him between

the forces of life and death. And since we've been referring back to my plays here, I might add that for
me as for most writers there is a perpetual mystery
cloaking man, this very same question as to what in
him so to speak drives him to death-dealing acts and
attitudes toward himself, and what decrees his stum-
bling search for what is life-giving. I often think that
is basically what I am writing about, and what my
morality consists in—I mean, of course, the moral
element in my plays. Incidentally, we spoke earlier of
masks. Masks are always to some degree frightening.
Because they speak of the dead, of death. They cover
what is alive and thus create a fundamental tension,
the fundamental tension. And in our time, as in others
in the past, the tension comes from the uncertainty as
to whether we are, in fact, nothing but the mask, the
representative of an interest, of a concealed or open
social necessity, mere switchboxes with turbine illusions. And there is undoubtedly a general fear,
conscious or not, that man as a unique thing is dis-
appearing or has already, but I don't think it comes
from nowhere, this fear. It is an inevitable part of the
contradiction that on the one hand we are trying to
make society rational, efficient, wasteless, and on the
other we extoll the individual. Progress, after all,
means ordering, at least as we commonly think of it,
while "man" in the best sense implies acts of private
judgment and will, self-expression, the personal and
individuated reaction to reality. Something has to
give. Up to this recent time it has been the individual
who has given, but now the reaction has set in. The
system of ordering itself is under attack. But the

strongest single idea that has come out of it is a wor-
ship of the irrational, as though in this is the protec-
tion of the individual. It is not, however, a promising
attitude. If only because the hippie, for example, does
depend on everybody else going to work on time, the
subways continuing to run, the food being raised in
an orderly fashion. A viable viewpoint, in other words,
has to include one's unspoken reliance on the garbage
being removed regularly. It must also include, and
have at its center, really, the fact that man deprived
of the habit of making real decisions is lessened and
can, as we know, effectively vanish.

EVANS: In this regard, you might find the actions
of one early behaviorist rather amusing. When John
B. Watson first began attacking the study of human
experience because it wasn't scientific, he used to challenge his detractors by the statement, "Prove that
you're conscious."

MILLER: Well, I can't prove that either. I'll speak
about what I know instead of about psychiatry, and
maybe it'll throw some light on psychology. I think
that the basic impulse of any writer is that, through
the process of writing, he speaks his own uniqueness.
By that I mean he deals with what he has discovered
himself. That means that nobody else has discovered
them, and that but for him, there wouldn't exist this
vision, this particular kind of style, this particular
kind of relationship he's talking about, if not the particular kind of moral he draws from the story. And
that reflects his own uniqueness. Now, what this has
to do with psychological work or science, I have no
idea. All I know is that the history of literature is so

long and evidently so fascinating to so many genera-
tions of peoples of all cultures that there must be
some validity in that quest. Possibly a way to understand the human being is to try to understand his own
concept of his uniqueness and his fear of its disap-
pearing.

EVANS: Then what you are saying is that creativity
is a form of the ultimate expression of uniqueness.
Therefore, by definition, this creative effort becomes
data that presumably will explain something about
what it is to be human.

MILLER: It is a kind of data. You see, I think we
tend to attack these problems at the later stages rather
than the earlier ones. I know a young man who is
about eighteen; I was talking to him a few weeks ago,
and the main questions were whether or not he should
go to college and what he should do, the usual crises
that people of that age go through, as all of us more
or less went through it. At one point he made a very
revealing remark. I said, "Why?" Tell me why do you
feel negative about pursuing any defined line in life,
whatever it might be." And he couldn't answer right
away, but later he said, "You know, I feel that everything has been done." He is by no means an incom-
petent person in any way, either with girls or studies
or anything else. Well, that's a hard one to answer.
Finally the thought went through my mind, and I said
to him, "You are you. There was never another guy
like you. There will never be another guy like you
again. You're like most people in most respects, but
in some one respect you aren't; in some small way
what you think and see is unique. There can only be

one of you." Well, it seemed to make a dent in him;
how deep a dent I don't know, but he seemed pleas-
antly shocked. To me, the striking thing was that he'd
gone through the American educational system for
eighteen years. He's been in school for thirteen years.
He's been reading and going to movies and the rest
of it. Now his thinking is an ideology, you see. It's
what he believes to be true about himself and the
world, and it's operating on him. It's the ideology, it
seems to me, of a kind of spiritual leveling or cancel-
ling-out which has been equated with realism. He has
been put into a position where he is trying, quite
against his own will, to fit in so much that finally he
can't see what will be left of him if he does fit in. And
he creates a kind of pause to live in. Incidentally, he
went not to a public school, but to a private school
that places special emphasis on psychological insights;
the teachers are in many cases analyzed people or
people highly conscious of psychology and psychiatry.
I think that what has happened with it all is that we
are "nothing-but" people. That is, whatever you feel
is "nothing-but" this or that kind of unconscious conflict, and the whole system reduces feelings to nullify-
ing, devaluating constructions. It started out as a good
idea. That is to say, you were relieving the guilt or
the anxiety of the people by saying, "Well, everybody
does this or feels this." Finally this kind of psychology
ended up I think by saying, "You are absolutely no
different from anybody else." So what the hell is the
use of living?

EVANS: Yes. You are touching on something here
which is important. Many writers and individuals in

the social sciences are expressing concern at the possibility that we are creating a culture of overconformity. Your example in terms of what was happening to this young man, his loss of identity in the morass of shaping forces, would seem to suggest your concern with this. As you know, of course, in recent years David Riesman dealt with this problem in his book, *The Lonely Crowd*, as did William White in *The Organization Man*. Erich Fromm, Otto Rank, and many other important thinkers in psychology in the last forty or fifty years have also been particularly concerned with this idea that man is being siphoned off. You have dealt with this theme in your work. Are there any particular characters in your plays, as you recall, who you think personify man caught up in this social shaping process and losing his identity and his individuality?

MILLER: I think that from that point of view you could find people in every play of mine who would come under that umbrella. If you start with *All My Sons*, the son, by overlooking his father's crime, is offered the chance to live a peaceful life without conflict. To be sure, there would be no justice. He would not have participated in a moral decision of some kind, but at the same time, he would have left that vision behind—that anger, that remorse, that pathos that he felt. He would have negated it by deadening it and himself. There is an instant where he was immediately connected to a social or moral or transcendent issue, namely the question of his own emotional attachment to the men he had led in the war, and it meant dying to that degree. The way it happens to

him is unique. And that uniqueness would have been
gone if he had chosen, if he had been able, to turn
himself away from what he conceived was necessary
to do. There is another example of this uniqueness
from the opposite direction, and that is in Willy
Loman. His individuality has nothing to do with such
an overt case of a wrong or social injustice in the
legal or even in the moral sense of the word. I think
what happens and what I was getting at in *Salesman,*
or what got me when I was writing the work, was an
implied simplicity, which is to be sure nostalgic and
romantic. Willy's father went across the country in a
covered wagon, and he made flutes. He wasn't anybody's employee nor anybody's boss; he was a free
man. He had a certain colorful character as opposed
to Willy, who stuck in Brooklyn and worked for a
company that was gradually trying to tell him that he
wasn't needed any more. His one claim to existence
was that he could sell, that the people on the road
knew him, that he was celebrated by the people on
the road, that he could park his car anywhere in New
England and cops would treat it like their own and
that the firm needed him. And suddenly this uniqueness is revealed as merely his economic function. It
turns out a mirage. In the meantime, he has foregone
in his life what he loved to do and what he was able
to do. In his case it happened to be working in con-
crete and painting the house and such things, all of
which have no social status whatsoever. His uniqueness was bypassed in favor of his total obedience to
social stimuli, and he ends up as he does in the play,
believing in what he is forced to rebel against. Simi-

larly, there is in *The Crucible* a man who is confronted with the opportunity, the possibility of negating himself, of calling true what he knows is half-truth. He's being asked to give way to his guilt, a guilt that arises because he has broken moral laws. By sinning that way, he's being asked by the court to condemn himself to a spiritual death. He can't finally do it. He dies a physical death, but he gains his soul, so to speak, he becomes his rebellion. In one way or another, I suppose, it is in all the plays. In *A View from the Bridge*, it takes place in still another context. A man has betrayed other people and then the desolation he feels inspires him to want to be destroyed. So what I'm positing in all this work, I suppose, is the secret existence of what used to be called an immortal soul, though I never thought of it in so many words. I would call it a unique identity of a moral kind. I admit that it's possible that it is simply a question of a consensus that over the ages, mainly through religion, the conception of a unique identity was instilled in man. We haven't the religion any more, so all we've got left is the arbitrary conception, which I admit is withering away at a great rate, but once it's given up, I think the game is up. Science will really be a game, a word game. It won't matter anymore because the subject will no longer be definable or visible; it will simply be a relationship of certain fairly obvious forces, and the human will simply be the adaptable.

EVANS: Erich Fromm uses the term "automaton-conformist" to describe the condition that you're describing here; when man becomes an automaton-conformist, he loses his identity and for all practical purposes, he's like a kind of instrument that's controlled by various forces.

MILLER: I often feel that man himself, the concept, is an act of will, an invention. It may have no natural existence and can be wiped out as man thought of himself in the past. It is an act of will which has to be engaged in by the intellectual class of the country because they are the heirs of it through their literature and through science itself, but they have to posit it not because it's provable but because it's necessary. Now that's on one level an unscientific statement, I suppose, but it's no more so than a physicist trying to measure something that is invisible and is engaged in mathematical calculations that would posit the existence of that something. Well, up to that point it's an act of will. He's asserting something for which there is no conceivable proof, and then he blows up a bomb and they say, "Well, you see it was always there." However, conceivably the bomb wouldn't blow up, or it wouldn't have for three hundred years. I've come to believe that positing man is as important as discovering him, and that's what I find missing, by the way, not only in psychology but in a lot of writing. The assumption is that one describes events, and that is scientific. Well, I don't believe anybody can be that above it all and remain open to human suffering, and truth itself. I would believe it if there were a class of gods who had no vested interest in man, but a scientist has that interest and if he hasn't, he's got an illusion to say the least.

EVANS: The underlying philosophical questions that you are raising concerning free will and determinism are regarded by many philosophers as being too abstract and circular to deal with meaningfully.

MILLER: I don't think it can be considered separately or abstractly, either. That's where this would be difficult to talk about. I think this way as a writer and probably I write plays because it is the only way I can really express this thought. I couldn't construct a play that would be persuasive or seem related to human life on the basis of free will, despite what I've just been saying. I believe that my concept of free will is a conditioned concept. Nevertheless, I didn't invent this. It came out of conflict and struggle. It is as if to say that if there weren't this element in us, the conception of what is not yet, I would not be interested in living. So therefore, it must be natural. Having an existence is as important as my blood supply. I think that in various situations where it is no longer really possible for people to conceive of something which is not yet, they become zombies. This is a common concentration camp syndrome. There were some individuals in the concentration camp who simply could no longer conceive of another situation. Would it be scientific to simply report this condition if it took over the world—and even to call it human nature?

EVANS: In this same vein, moving I think through Willy, in *Death of a Salesman*, you share with us brilliantly the existential problems of aging. It might be interesting to relate your insights to the experiences of many psychotherapists. When asked, "Why are you seeking psychotherapy?" some aging patients will say, "Well, I don't know what I'm living for. I don't know what the purpose of all this is. I'm not even sure who I am." This question is not generally asked by the individual until he actually sees himself as aging, but is otherwise well established in life. However, perhaps ninety percent of the population is still concerned with satisfying needs more primitive than those of self-actualization; they apparently do not, at least overtly, face existential dilemmas. They never come to grips with the question. According to your definition, then, these people do not exist.

MILLER: The old, like the unskilled, are unnecessary to the production apparatus. I've never come across a study of the similarities in the viewpoints of both these classes, but I'd bet there are many. But the unskilled unemployed don't get into the hands of psychotherapists. I wouldn't be surprised, though, if they asked the same existential questions as they aged. I know that back in the Depression it was a common thing to hear an unemployed man conjuring up what in better hands would be called fundamental questions of the meaning of existence. A sense of futility can have many roots and aging is only the most obvious, and probably the most pathetic. Actually, though, Willy doesn't quite fit into this category, at least in my eyes. He discovers he is unneeded anymore, but what he is reaching for is something like a token of immortality, a sign that he lived. You might call it some affirmation by others of the values for which he struggled. This demand is not confined to the old, they merely illuminate by the desperation of the Last Days, so to speak, what is eating people of any age group. I want to say something contradictory, though. Obviously I see people as being intensely conditioned by what society does to them. But the interior geography of man doesn't change very much, I think, from one period to another. Different virtues are prized at different times, of course—the emphasis differs as to what makes a man valuable, evil, worthy, and so on. But if you read through the testimony of the Salem Witchcraft Trials, for instance, you will come on the common sexual fantasies, repressions, symbolizations, and so forth that we are so aware of today. In other words, the sociological attack is very limited if you are looking for some way of understanding what goes into making a man. Something quite permanent and unchanging persists in him through all the systems that have sought to control him. There is a continuity in us which goes back into Egypt, into the beginnings. My point is that there is such a thing as Man, or at least a matrix that conditioning cannot wholly surround and quench. This would demand a certain humility in the use of any analytic technique. In recent years we've seen the resistance of this creature in the Eastern countries, for example, and now through the rebellions of youth and the Negro in our own country. The creature is not wholly malleable after all. I'd even go so far as to say that perhaps part of his difficulty in changing—even for the better—is his instinct to protect his repetitious human definition.

EVANS: Earlier, Jung's notion of archetypes was introduced into our discussion. As you recall, Jung developed the concept to suggest that there were pervasive behavior potentials in man that cut through time

and various cultures, and to understand these potentials, you must go back to man's early beginning. In a
sense, you're again pointing to the validity of Jung's
notion of archetypes.

MILLER: I think that the proof is that you can read
literature from older cultures that are absolutely di-
vorced from ours and have nothing in common with it,
and you see a parade of individuals who with the
slightest superficial changes are people who are walk-
ing around today. Now that kind of information is
irreproachable because the man putting it down had
no interest in proving anything of the kind that we're
talking about.

EVANS: Yes, it is quite fascinating. But let me just
take another approach to what you're saying. Jung
and many other scholars with historical perspective
have tried to look at the problems as you do. But yet
modern cultural anthropologists, who emphasize cultural determinism, believe that we are what we are
as a function of the specific culture in which we develop and that cultural influence can be modified. For
example, Margaret Mead has done a very interesting
study of how an entire culture in New Guinea changed
almost overnight when Americans brought their values
into the culture. You may be familiar with this work.

MILLER: Yes, I am.

EVANS: What is your opinion of it? Do you think
that these changes might actually be superficial?

MILLER: Let me say this, and don't laugh. Superficial changes can be decisive, in the sense that I
could see where a superficial change in a culture
would increase the supply of people to that culture;

for example, a superficial change like the introduction
of penicillin or teaching a midwife to wash her hands
just before she's going to deliver a baby. That doesn't
take much changing, just a bar of soap. But it can
make an island overpopulated and even start wars,
which in turn demand character changes in people,
military rather than peacetime virtues, a paranoid
fearfulness rather than trust and confidence. What
I'm driving at, I suppose, is a synthetic approach to
man, that is to say, the virtue that I finally see in
literature and its value apart from the literary or
esthetic value is that to me it's the one way a man has
found to synthesize all his insides in a dynamic fashion,
so that it defends us against doing what so many
psychological systems fall into doing, and that is to
partition people. That makes it much more difficult,
I admit, to draw conclusions about what makes people
tick. But I still say that you have to keep your eye on
your source material, namely man and his most immediate reflection that I know about, his art, his literature. Given Freud or anybody else, it is still the best
picture, the best and most analytical, if you will,
source of insight and wisdom into men because it is
the only one that attempts to synthesize the various
aspects of human life; the greater the literature, the
greater variety of the forces it brings into play. Now,
Shakespeare was a great writer not only because he
was a poet, which is part of what I'm about to say,
but because a character in his play is the product of
his past, his present, his individual nature, his immediate conflict, and numerous other forces. And that
dynamic quality is the reality. I'm worried, in effect,

by some of the attempts that I hear about from time to time to pick out of this complex group of forces one or two or three or four which it is said will control man. I'm worried not only because it isn't true, but it might distract people dangerously for a time. That is to say, men are very impressionable, and if they think something is true, they act accordingly. They'll even take on a neurosis suggested to them, and one has to be very responsible toward people when one suggests certain things about them, and says this is why people act. When I was a kid, I remember there was a thing called the inferiority complex to which I believe you referred in another context earlier in our discussion. I knew nothing about anything but I clearly recall that everybody suddenly discovered that he had an inferiority complex and that was the basis of both his success and his failure; of course, you can make a great case out of it. I think one of the reasons we even have this conversation is that culture in terms of the deep and steady use of literature is so sparse in this country. I think in a way psychology is trying to fill a gap. We're creating a psychological culture in the sense that other countries have created a literary or artistic culture.

EVANS: In this respect, I think you have raised a very interesting point: you're proposing that this ego, this will, or whatever makes man at least partially self-determined is a very fragile thing, and psychologists might be perfectly capable of destroying this in the individual through some systematically applied behavioral shaping or controlling techniques of the sort we discussed earlier.

MILLER: I think it is possible, at least for a time. Sometimes it can have more than academic or even literary ramifications, such as the problem of juvenile delinquency in this country. I spent a few months in the streets of New York in 1957, thinking I would someday write about juvenile delinquency, and I went through the usual sources. I always like to know what anybody else knows about something before I decide what I know about it or before I decide that I know anything about it. In this case I had never been a juvenile delinquent, but I had been brought up in Harlem and I knew a little about them just from my childhood experience. I had a head start there, but that was all. I talked with sociologists and psychiatrists and psychologists, many of whom were working on this problem directly for the city in one respect or another, mostly formal projects but some simply out of personal interest. Now, if you talk to the cultural anthropologist from Columbia, you've got one picture of why they were delinquent and what had to be done about it. If you talked to psychologists, you got another picture. If you talked to psychiatrists, you got still another one, and if you talked to a sociologist, you got a fourth or fifth one. Finally, I realized that my view was probably as good or as bad but certainly no worse than theirs. All I knew was that one element was missing from the whole business. These kids had been conceived as having entered some new area of human behavior. A new world had been created from which nondelinquents were barred. They were in a special category now. They were juvenile delinquents, and they were being observed that way. At one point, out of desperation, we had a meeting to which I called about ten people, and they attended it because they really, at bottom, were desperate. After all their personality theories had been stated, they really were getting nowhere because they could not change the society. You couldn't psychoanalyze all the jokers in that neighborhood, but if you could, would you want to?—to make them learn to tolerate the intolerable? That is, I think, a good example of the synthetic approach or the want of it; by "synthetic" I mean a way of thinking that brings all the elements of a situation together, as opposed to an analysis that pulls things apart and leaves them in pieces.

EVANS: Who was in the group that you called together?

MILLER: Well, they represented various disciplines. By this time they were all humble if not humiliated by their failure to affect anything except individuals here and there among the delinquent kids. The idea was that they were about to set up Mobilization for Youth, which was, as you know, an attempt in New York City not only to do something but to measure the results of what they were doing. And as I've told you, I know nothing about sociological procedures or the rest of it, and all I knew was what I observed by sticking around and trying to write about it; I emphasize trying to write about it, because by just observing it, you don't arrive at that high attention of really trying to symbolize the meaning of something. It seemed to me that what was really missing in the kids was not only a sense that they could join society, which is a general way of putting it, but that it was possible to give them the responsibility for themselves in society right now, not someday when they were cured or when they would grow up and be nice fellows and keep their noses clean and go to college and become lawyers. I said, "Suppose they live in bad housing and go around in gangs of fifty or sixty, why not give up telling them not to break the windows in the housing project, or not to do this or not to do that or offering them examples of a good father in terms of the social worker, or any of those methods? Instead, why not give them the idea of protesting so that they really get in trouble with the authorities, not as patients, not as an exercise, but as a social movement." Because it had occurred to me that I was brought up during the Depression where I wandered around with a lot of guys who broke windows and stole things. And one of the big things that happened that I thought might have reduced what we call delinquent acts in these kids was that they got a sense that they could protest their condition through a social movement, through some combined action. That made them social beings, curiously enough, because their point of view was directed toward society instead of the opposite direction. Well, Mobilization for Youth did this. Or it attempted to do this in a faltering and rather frightened way. They opened their premises to people who had started a rent strike because of the abysmal conditions in which they were living; they refused to pay any more rent. They allowed them to use their mimeograph machine. They didn't supply actual leadership because they were prohibited from doing so by their charter, but they inevitably had to provide some

if the people wanted to protest. And they did not regard it as a delinquent action. The result was just as
I must say I predicted in the beginning. I'd said, "If
you're really doing well, you're going to get in trouble
with the police department and the mayor and everybody else. If you're not accomplishing anything, everybody's going to say you're great." And sure enough,
as soon as the protest became serious, Mobilization
for Youth was stripped of autonomy and forced to
conform. Now the alternative to this was what? All
the psychiatrists had said that we'd need six thousand
analysts for this neighborhood alone. It would presumably take at least two years to analyze each kid.
Well, I'll stop right there because obviously, you can't
do that. So we get back to my original proposition,
which was that in order to proceed even scientifically
in this respect, one had to knowingly inject a judgment of the value of certain ideas as opposed to others.
In my view, which was not a separated and completely
esthetic or judicial judgment, there was a value, a
human value, in opening up the road to protest. I
think protesting is a healing mechanism, and I think
people who have lost it or have been prohibited from
using it are losing some of their identity. Now in those
few cases where the people accomplished something,
their pride returned, their sense of being citizens of
the city of New York returned. Suddenly power that
had completely overwhelmed them before to the point
where they had contempt for it was something they
too could now participate in and even manipulate,
even cause it to recognize their existence. And they
began to exist as unique human beings, in the most

primitive way imaginable, of course, but this was never carried through, and God knows what would have happened if it had. But in other words, I think that there is a humanistic premise that I believe science cannot set aside; if it does, it will truly cease to be science either.

EVANS: I think your example of delinquency is an excellent one because to some degree, this becomes the battleground for these value systems. Perhaps naïvely applied theories of significant social thinkers such as Durkheim and Marx have had a tremendous effect on social welfare agencies and resulted in a strong commitment to social determinism; that is, if you can change social conditions and relieve the physical and economic plight of the individual, you also change him in the process. In a delinquency project similar to Mobilization for Youth in which we were involved, we concluded that one of the dangers in some well-meaning social welfare activity predicated on a naïve social determinism is that instead of necessarily solving a person's problem over the long run, imposed social change may merely breed greater dependency in him. The alternative is investing some responsibility in the individual, or as you put it, at least begin with some sense of the capacity to protest. As the direction of the recent protest movements has indicated, there is a very fine balance however, isn't there? That is, it's a risky thing.

MILLER: That's another point, by the way. I sense in some of these approaches a fear of risk, a fear of risking freedom. What right have you got to tell kids that they have any less right to protest their condition

than people who live in a good neighborhood, who
certainly are not going to sit there and do nothing
when their conditions become dreadful. Why do you
say that others have the right and these kids don't?
You see, these differentials communicate themselves.
In other words, I believe that a delinquent has
learned to be a delinquent. Somebody has taught him
to be a delinquent. Delinquents are not born; they're
made. And I hate to use that dreadful word, society,
but I mean by that us and what we think is the way
out, not just the gangsters and real estate owners who
don't take care of their property. Those kids were
given a certain message over many years by social
workers: they were told they were delinquent. This is
not to be discounted because the slums are full of
social workers; they are the delinquent's sole contact
with the so-called respectable world.

EVANS: Your point reminds me of a scene in *West
Side Story* which satirizes this notion of shifting responsibility away from the self. The juvenile delinquents are with Police Officer Krupke. They taunt
him in song that they aren't responsible for their delinquent behavior but social conditions are. It would
be interesting to see the kind of play that you would
create from your experience. Had you begun speculat-
ing in terms of characterization in a play about this
problem?

MILLER: Yes. I started out to do a screenplay. You
see, I was approached by people from the New York
City Youth Board, which was a city-financed attempt
to develop methods of dealing with what was then
the big problem, gang fighting. It has since become

dope, which is the opposite of gang fighting; it's complete acquiescence. Dope addiction is the total victory
of conformism. The object at that time, in the middle
fifties, was to stop the warfare. I got interested in it
only because I knew nothing about it, and I thought
that I would be interested in seeing what was happening right under my nose, but also hoped that a movie
could be developed out of it. But what happened over
a period of months was that I began to see the obvious,
namely that the people who were operating the project were at sea. It wasn't as though I was confronted
with a solution and could show its operation among
delinquents and how they were saved. I felt finally
that the savers needed saving as much as the kids did.
I started the script on the first basis and broke off because I realized I had nothing to say in this respect,
nor did anybody else, and consequently, I spent four
months in the street trying to find out what it was
clear nobody could tell me. Nobody knew. And I came
up with the solution I just told you. It isn't a solution,
but at least it was a way in which to approach the
whole problem. It was finally tried to a degree, and
was slugged to death by the city administration. In
the process, I got involved personally in a minor side
drama which helped to abort that particular project
at the time; the emissaries of the House Un-American
Activities Committee went down to the city of New
York secretly and told them that if they had anything
to do with me, they would be sorry, so that I was
offered the project provided my name didn't appear
on it, which I somehow connected with the whole
question of juvenile delinquency, except that this was

adult delinquency. I refused to adopt anonymity or pledge allegiance and got into a big fight with the city. The end of it was that I got out of the project. But someday I might do something about the problem again. I don't know.

EVANS: We've been talking about significant problems, but an even greater threat to man is nuclear war. On one occasion during a conference I attended, Sir Julian Huxley drew a very large thermometer. He drew a high boiling point on this thermometer and said that it represented the technological growth and development which lead to the nuclear war potential that would enable man to destroy himself. Then he checked a very low below freezing point on the thermometer and said that it indicated the progress men have made in understanding one another. He said the gap is so great that we may have little hope of overcoming it. But this gap between social psychological communication and understanding and technological development must be closed if man is not to be destroyed. In the discussions I've had as part of our National Science Foundation project with the world's notable contributors to psychology, these men have generally responded to this question of this gap by suggesting that if we look at this problem in a purely detached and rational manner, we certainly will have to conclude that man will probably destroy himself. Yet they generally go on to maintain that this very cynical belief might lead to a self-fulfilling prophecy. So faith and hope must be maintained, that this gap between a potentially destructive technology and man's capability for coping with it will be overcome. How do you feel about this problem?

MILLER: First of all, I have no doubt that we are
capable of dropping another atom bomb, this time on
Vietnam. There is a species of thinking which regards
the bomb as merely an intensification of TNT. We
could do this because we are politically in bank-
ruptcy in Vietnam; we have put into power and linked
our prestige to a junta which obviously has no significant popular following. We have done the same thing
for a century in Central America, Cuba, and Hawaii,
the Philippines, and other places. The difference this
time is that we arrived late—after a nationalist movement had matured in Vietnam which is not having
any of this. The problem is that our military is having
to admit that it has not won a war; our aircraft and
armaments technologists and industrial experts are
having to admit that all their destructiveness has not
broken the will of naked peasants. Politically, our
geopoliticians are having to admit the limits of American power. Internally, we are having to admit that
the beneficence of our salvationism is brutal underneath. But all of this has come about contingent on
one fact—that if we drop a bomb the world itself
may end. Science, therefore, challenges us to a new—
and very old—vision. The vision of man humiliated
in his pride, humiliated and made more wise by the
oncoming, stubborn, immortal nature of man himself,
of man and his limits. I, no more than anyone else,
am by any means sure we won't "solve" the problem
by the ultimate refusal to recognize those limits and
that barren pride, solve the problem by splattering
the planet into the heavens. But I knowingly engage
in an act of will, that's all. It is an act based on
biological imperatives but willful nevertheless because

I could also choose to believe that we will never destroy the world, only Vietnam, and go about my business perhaps somewhat depressed, but hoping that someday we will be allowed to rehabilitate that poor country, or some guilt-offering of the sort. I believe that man is indeed capable of the ultimate in destruction; therefore, I can only will that it not come to pass. What basis is there for such willfulness? For one thing, the refusal of the Vietnamese to give up under our immense superiority in arms, before our myth. If they can stand up to it on the battlefield, we can and must stand up to it here, where it is far less dangerous. But it is also that in all our stupidity, our mendaciousness, our self-generated illusions about what we do, there is a powerful desire to help, to live in peace and so forth. It is not a question of being optimistic but of recognizing the dialectic and of choosing which side of it one will lend one's strength to. I am perfectly aware that a point arrives where people are incapable of resisting irrational aggressive behavior, total destruction. It is not despite but because of that that I feel as I do—because the resistance to it is also a fact, a possibility equally real.

EVANS: What you're saying is quite consistent with the work of Neal Miller and John Dollard in their theory of frustration-aggression. They proposed the theory that all frustration leads to aggression. Thus the very act of stifling aggression produces more frustration which leads to more aggression. Police action against rioters has illustrated this. You're suggesting this same idea, more or less.

MILLER: My point here is that anyone who really

and truly wants peace has got to beware of the threshold beyond which it is dialectically impossible any
longer to stop short of total war. I think we are drawing very close to that point in Vietnam, where with
the best will in the world, the wisest politicians might
still be saying that it is to our interest not to fight a
total war, but they would be incapacitated by the
public feeling in relation to this thing which they
themselves have inflamed.

EVANS: Now, in a way, the characters in your plays
illustrate the plight of man and his responsibility and
guilt, but here you feel that the mechanism has already been set in motion so that by rational analysis,
you think we will probably have a nuclear war before
too many years.

MILLER: I would say yes, I think so. And yet I
think it need not be if certain lessons are learned
objectively and léarned now. I see no alternative but
to try to teach those lessons and for people to try to
learn them. And that is that we are very fragile beings.
We are not in control of ourselves beyond a certain
threshold. I know people right now who know as much
as I do about Vietnam who feel that it is a fruitless
war and something that will not ultimately redound
to our profit, and yet they say, "Well, we're in it, and
therefore we must go on with it." And you say, "Why?"
Well, then you get into an area of irrationality. It's
quite obvious it's irrational. Why should it not be true
that the greatness and honor of the United States
would not be enhanced by the President's saying,
"Look, we have despite everything been drawn into a
dreadful error. And this country is great enough to

say that we will not compound the error at the sacri-
fice of the lives of millions of people." It seems to me
that's a new definition of what man is, of what honor
is, but at the same time people would understand,
even welcome it.

EVANS: Yes, I think that you're raising the question
of circularity. Of course, various psychological research findings suggest that attitudes are not really
based on information or fact but are basically irrational. In fact, it is very difficult to find any support
for the presence of truly rational belief systems, attitudes, and values in most people. So how can you ask
rationality of man, who may be in the final analysis
an irrational creature?

MILLER: That gets to a thing that I wanted to talk
about, and that is, we think about everything except
what is happening. The fact that underlies my feeling
in this respect is that a large number of people who
are neither Communist, capitalist, or anything else
but just people are being destroyed here, and that includes our own men. I'm sure if we took a poll of the
dead, their political opinions for the most part would
be unrelated to this whole so-called issue, except for
the cadres of leadership of the Viet Cong, who I'm
sure are in the minority in Vietnam as they are in
every country. Most people are not politically inspired.
Now as a playwright, my first question is, "What is
happening?" I've used different terminology in the
past; I've said that people have masks and that the
purpose of drama is to tear away those masks, but
perhaps a better way of putting it is that we all have
illusions about what we are doing, what the other

person is doing, what the nature of the conflict is. The drama works best when I present what I call in the first act the "visible reality." The audience nods to itself and says, "Yes, that's the way it is." And then gradually, I turn the scene around until I show them that maybe that is not the way it is, that what it appears to be is sometimes directly contradictory to what it is. And what we need is a Grand Dramatist in this world who would possibly be able to do that. Unfortunately, the cast of characters is too big.

EVANS: Well, Mr. Miller, we had an opportunity to discuss some of your masterful works from a psychological perspective and hopefully have given psychologists and nonpsychologists alike a great deal to think about. May I ask, where do you go from here?

MILLER: Well, it's hard to describe; I'll be able to tell you better when I've done them. I can't answer that question rationally or schematically. In general, I find myself trying to make human relations felt between individuals and the larger structure of the world. This kind of relationship is particularly invisible to me, particularly difficult to touch or to formulate, and yet I think it can be. By the larger world I mean the political world, the social world, the world of war and peace. The humanities are falteringly trying to create an irreducible image of what it means to be human. You see, there is either a concentration on psychological behavior or depersonalized social metaphors, and frankly, I am not any longer preoccupied with that kind of partitioning. The totality is always the great challenge. To me the problem is man as a creature in a universe which he knows somewhere in his head is moving him, which he can't seem to reach even as he is altering it as never before. I think the world has to strive toward an opening of consciousness of man as the center, a way to reach beyond conditioning so that after all decisions are made, and necessity has its hour, we will go on to ask ourselves, "What happens to people here?" Even necessity is only what we believe it to be. It ends up basically an esthetic problem to me, a question of unity, of form. You see, my mind goes back to Elizabethan drama where the lines of connection between the state, the polity, the habits of the king, and what went on with the gravedigger were strong lines. We have no structure for his kind of connection. We have to synthesize or formulate one. We have to invest on the stage the connections that finally make the whole. For they exist, however concealed they may be.

EVANS: Maybe so, Mr. Miller, but in our discussion you certainly have formulated many fascinating connections—both positive and negative—between your ideas and those of psychology. You have given me very forthright and honest reactions to some very complicated questions, and have not shirked any of them. Thank you very much.

The Dialogue Format—
An Innovation in
Instruction

Judging from reactions we have received, the inclusion of a perspective on these books as an innovation in teaching appears to be of value to readers. Thus we again present such a perspective in this volume.

The present book constitutes the fifth in a series based primarily on dialogues with some of the world's outstanding contributors to personality psychology. Because of our belief that Arthur Miller's drama reflects a profound contribution to personality psychology that is unmatched in more formal psychological writing, we felt that its inclusion in this series would constitute an interesting departure.

Designed as an instructional innovation as well as content of general interest, the series was launched in 1957 with completion of such dialogues with the late Carl Jung and Ernest Jones supported by a grant from the Fund for the Advancement of

APPENDIX 1

Education, and is being continued under a current grant from the National Science Foundation. A basic purpose of the project is to produce for teaching purposes a series of films recording these dialogues which introduce the viewer to our distinguished interviewees' major contributions to the fund of personality psychology and human behavior. It is our hope that these films will also serve as historical documents of increasing value as significant contributions to the history of the behavioral sciences.[1]

The volumes in this series are based on edited transcripts of the dialogue which include the text of additional audiotaped discussions as well as the content of the films. It is our hope that these dialogues in the print medium will extend the primary goals of the films: (1) to introduce the reader to the contributor's major ideas and points of view; (2) to convey through the extemporaneousness of the dialogue style a feeling for the personality of the contributor.

An attempt is made to emphasize spontaneity in our interaction with our participants; this we feel adds a dimension to the project that is not usually present in more didactic forms of teaching. Yet, although these encounters are extemporaneous, we are hopeful that this does not detract from any significance that the content may have. We would hope that a relatively informal discussion with an outstanding contributor to a discipline, as he seriously examines his own work, will not be of less significance by virtue of its informality.

[1] The films are distributed by Association Instructional Films, 600 Madison Avenue, New York, New York 10022.

A more detailed description of the philosophy and techniques of this project is reported elsewhere (in press). However, a few points bearing on the content of this volume might be emphasized here. The questions are not intended to deal with all of Arthur Miller's work. Since selectivity was necessary in developing the questions so that the discussion can be completed within a limited time interval, it would not be fair to say the results of these sessions—either in the films, which reflect the content emanating from only about half the time spent with the participant, or even in the books, which reflect about twice the amount of time—necessarily provide the basis for an inclusive summary of the contributor's work. I would feel that the purpose of this project has been realized if I am perceived as having merely provided a perhaps novel medium—a psychological frame of reference— through which Arthur Miller can express his views.

Trends in Personality Psychology Relating to the Dialogue

Rather than attempt to summarize all of the major psychological concepts presented in the dialogue as we did in the volumes based on Jung and Fromm, I shall again—as I did in the Erikson and Skinner volumes—take the liberty of briefly presenting frameworks which I find valuable in teaching personality theory to students, hoping they may in turn be of value to the reader of this book in comprehending the backdrop against which we may look at my discussion with Arthur Miller. It should be emphasized that Arthur Miller is included in this series because he can in a sense be called a "personality psychologist," because of the many insights he presents which parallel particularly contemporary humanistic psychology and psychoanalysis.

There are three frameworks around which I believe current approaches to personality can be analyzed in order to help to

APPENDIX 2

locate any theoretical position within the matrix of general personality theory. These frameworks are really descriptive approaches to the understanding of personality which develop theoretically from basic orientations focusing around biological determinism, cultural determinism, or self-determinism.

One group of contributors, apparently emphasizing biological determinism, has been considered more or less traditionally psychoanalytical. It includes such writers as Hans Sachs and Ernest Jones, as well as Freud himself. This group has been characterized as emphasizing what Freud called "repetition compulsion," a concept which maintains that the first five years of life, which are strongly influenced by biological propensities, are very important in human development because they set the stage for and determine a life style which is manifested continuously throughout the individual's lifetime; central to this postulate is the notion of the Oedipal complex. Another important aspect of traditional Freudian theory was brought out by Ernest Jones in our earlier published dialogue with him (Evans, 1964), in which he unabashedly makes the statement, "Well, man is, after all, an animal." Some people think that this is a cynical view, although Jones denied that Freud was inordinately cynical. Freud's earliest picture of man is that of an organism dominated to a large degree by its id—the animal, biological side of him—against which the ego —the conscious, the self of man—is fighting a tough battle. He is seen as just barely able to hold his head above water in the struggle to keep from being drowned by the animal he basically is. This view of man, as articulated in Freud's early works, was also accepted by many of the early followers of Freud. With Freud, they believe that the center of man's motivation and energy is the sexual libido, which to them was a manifestation of the dominant animal aspect of man. Although Freud in his later work began to emphasize other aspects of man's makeup also, many thinkers continue to perceive the classical psychoanalytical position in terms of these early views of Freud. Actually, the above description is probably a vast oversimplification of Freud's view, as Fromm and Erikson, for example, implied in our earlier volumes.

Another group of contributors, the neo-Freudians, has placed more stress on the effects of cultural influences on man's development. To the neo-Freudians, the early Freudians would appear to have taken too seriously the notion that the instinctual animal nature, the repetition compulsion, and a general biological patterning of early development is found *universally,* and that these elements dominate man's nature. The neo-Freudians take exception to this concept of universality. They believe that man is primarily a product of the specific kind of culture in which he lives, and that learning plays a much more important part than does biological patterning in the development of personality.

The late Karen Horney, for example, a prominent neo-Freudian who had been with the Berlin Psychoanalytic Institute, became so disturbed by many notions in the biological orientation of the early Freudian position, such as the postulation of male superiority (evidenced by the assertion that penis envy was characteristic of women) that she broke away from the orthodox Freudian position. She developed a view that man is shaped to significant extent by the society with which he must cope when he deals with the anxieties of reality. She considered this anxiety produced by societal pressures more important in shaping man than his anxiety about overcoming his basic biological animal nature.

Again, as indicated in one of our earlier volumes (Evans, 1966c), although Fromm does not like the label neo-Freudian, he too certainly takes exception to Freud's emphasis on the Oedipal situation so central to Freud's "biological unfolding" view of man's development.

Other psychologists have attempted to place man within his social milieu, in the belief that it constitutes the essential force in shaping personality. In spite of the fact that Freud later appeared to be placing more emphasis on the importance of society as a formative influence in the development of individual personality, traditional Freudian theory as it is most often expounded does not emphasize this element. The neo-Freudians made dominant this aspect of man's relationship to his world, emphasizing a cultural determinism which constitutes a departure from what is customarily regarded as traditional Freudian theory. Had Freud emphasized this aspect of the relationship earlier in his writings, he might not have acquired the reputation for being so biologically oriented. At any rate, many of his immediate followers certainly perpetuated a biological orientation, whereas the neo-Freudians, represented by Horney, Abram Kardiner, and Harry Stack Sullivan, deviated from that point of view. The neo-Freudian group challenged psychoanalysis to extend the study of man at least beyond Freud's early basic tenets.

Another characteristic of the neo-Freudian group is evident in their techniques of psychotherapy. The older Freudians considered psychotherapy a five-day-a-week affair which takes from three to five years of intensive therapy before it can be successful; the neo-Freudians, utilizing recent innovations, believe that situational factors are much more important, and claim to have achieved results with much shorter periods of psychotherapy.

Somewhere between the neo-Freudians and the traditional Freudians there is a group of three significant individuals whom we might describe as Freudian dissentients; for although each of them worked closely with Freud, each subsequently broke with him or was repudiated by him for one reason or another. Carl Jung, Otto Rank, and Alfred Adler would be included in this group.

By all accounts, Adler's early work placed the primary emphasis on the social man, and it might be said that Adler set the stage for the emergence of the neo-Freudian group. In a different direction, although many of his ideas about early biological conceptions were in agreement with Freud's, Rank's preoccupation with the "will" and its development of autonomy introduced a type of self-determinism that Freud apparently did not emphasize.

As became apparent in our dialogue with Carl Jung, he had moved away from Freud's basic tenets, while retaining Freud's idea of the unconscious, expanding it into a race and individual unconscious and incorporating into the race unconscious Freud's early notion of archetypes, developing this concept beyond Freud's postulation. However, with this central conception of individuation Jung also moved away from the emphasis on biological determinism. Jung, perhaps more profoundly than either Adler or Rank, turned toward the idea of the development of an ultimately self-determined spiritual being which transcends the biological forces acting on man. This led him to consider many metaphysical conceptions, obviously not in keeping with present-day notions of a scientific pyschology.

As indicated in the introduction to the present volume as the position most paralleling Arthur Miller's, a great deal of thought today continues to reflect the greater concern for man's individuality and self-responsibility than is found in either biological or cultural determinism. For example, the position of the existentialists—particularly in the works of Rollo May, the distinguished philosophical theologian Paul Tillich, the philosophers Husserl and Heidegger, and the work of Carl Rogers in the United States—reflects this concern, as does the work of Abraham Maslow (1954) in recent years. Obviously many other psychologists have currently reflected an increased concern with the autonomy of the self, for example, Allport and McCurdy.

However, it must be kept in mind that related to any theoretical discussion of "determinism" and personality theory, the behavioristic orientation may still be perhaps the most significant theoretical reference group for American academic and research psychologists. As the leading exponent of this view, B. F. Skinner interprets not merely cultural influences in a broad sense, but the immediate environment in a narrow sense as being the significant shaping force on the individual. As environment is controlled experimentally and even in the clinical situation to modify behavior in a desired direction, very few assumptions concerning the "internal workings" of personality have to be made.

Questions in the dialogue were designed to obtain reactions from Miller concerning the three orientations described above, as well as relating his views to the behavioristic orientation more specifically, since it is obvious that this view would be most antithetical, thus most provocative to Miller.

At various points in the dialogue Arthur Miller was given an opportunity to deal directly or indirectly with the differences among the three positions represented by the biological, the cultural, and the self-deterministic points of view. I believe we can say that in his work social and self-determinism are more important than any of the other positions. However, perhaps most significant of all, Miller, as so many of our most creative individuals, refuses to be strictly categorized at all.

RECOMMENDED
READINGS

Adler, A. *Understanding Human Nature*. (Translated by W. B. Wolfe.) New York: Greenberg, 1927.

Allport, G. W. *Pattern and Growth in Personality*. New York: Holt, Rinehart & Winston, 1961.

Evans, R. I. *B. F. Skinner: An introduction to the man and his ideas*. New York: E. P. Dutton, 1968.

—————. *Conversations with Carl Jung and Reactions from Ernest Jones*. New York: D. Van Nostrand, 1964.

—————. *Dialogue with Erich Fromm*. New York: Harper & Row, 1966.

—————. *Dialogue with Erik Erikson*. New York: Harper & Row, 1967.

—————. "Filmed Dialogues with Notable Contributors to Psychology." *Psychological Reports*, in press.

Evans, R. I. & Leppmann, P. K. *Resistance to Innovation in Higher Education*. San Francisco: Jossey-Bass, 1968.

Freud, A. *The Ego and The Mechanism of Defense*. New York: International University Press, 1946.

Heidegger, M. *An Introduction to Metaphysics*. (Translated by R. Manheim.) New Haven, Conn.: Yale University Press, 1959.

Horney, K. *The Neurotic Personality of Our Time*. New York: W. W. Norton, 1937.

Husserl, E. *Ideas: General Introduction to Pure Phenomenology*. (Translated by W. R. Boyce.) New York: Macmillan, 1952.

Jones, E. *The Life and Work of Sigmund Freud*. Vol. 1. New York: Basic Books, 1953.

Kant, I. *Critique of Pure Reason*. (Translated by Norman Kemp Smith.) London: Macmillan, 1929.

McClelland, D. "Psychoanalysis and Religious Mysticism" in *The Roots of Consciousness*. New York: D. Van Nostrand, 1964.

McCurdy, H. G. *The Personal World: An Introduction to the Study of Personality*. New York: Harcourt, Brace & World, 1961.

Maslow, A. H. *Motivation and Personality*. New York: Harper & Row, 1954.

May, R. "Existential Bases of Psychotherapy" in *Existential Psychology*, Rollo May (Ed.), New York: Random House, 1961.

Murray, H. A. *Explorations in Personality*. New York: Oxford University Press, 1938.

Pavlov, I. P. *Conditioned Reflexes*. London: Oxford University Press, 1927.

Riesman, D. *The Lonely Crowd*. New Haven, Conn.: Yale University Press, 1950.

Rogers, C. R. *Casebook of Non-directive Counseling*. Boston: Houghton Mifflin, 1947.

Sanford, N. "Will Psychologists Study Human Problems?" *Amer. Psychol.*, 1965, Vol. 20, No. 3, 192-202.

Skinner, B. F. *Walden Two*. New York: Macmillan, 1948.

Sullivan, H. S. *The Interpersonal Theory of Psychiatry*. New York: W. W. Norton, 1953.

Tillich, P. *The Courage to Be*. New Haven, Conn.: Yale University Press, 1952.

INDEX